A Practical Guide to Teaching Physical Education in the Secondary School

This practical and accessible workbook is designed to support student physical education teachers as they develop their basic teaching skills, and increase their broader knowledge and understanding for teaching physical education. Newly qualified and beginning teachers should also find it useful.

A Practical Guide to Teaching Physical Education in the Secondary School provides a wealth of practical activities and materials, underpinned by relevant evidence/theory, which have been developed through the authors' vast experience of working with student teachers. These activities provide opportunities to analyse learning and performance. The book has been designed to be written in directly, and so provide a useful record of progress. Case studies are also included, as are examples of existing good practice and a range of tried-and-tested strategies.

The book has been written to complement *Learning to Teach Physical Education in the Secondary School: A Companion to School Experience, 2nd edition* (edited by Susan Capel), and can be used to reinforce some of the basic teaching skills covered in that textbook. However, the book can also be used equally successfully as a stand-alone text. It has been designed to be used by student teachers, on their own or with others, or by school- or university-based tutors with their student teachers, to develop and/or reinforce their understanding of some of the important aspects of learning to teach physical education.

Susan Capel is Professor and Head of School of Sport and Education at Brunel University, UK. She was President of the Physical Education Association of the UK from 2001 to 2003. **Peter Breckon** is Course Leader of the BSc Secondary Education and Physical Education, Brunel University, UK. **Jean O'Neill** is Senior Lecturer in Physical Education, Chelsea School of PE, Sports Science, Dance and Leisure, University of Brighton, UK.

Routledge Teaching Guides
Series Editors: Susan Capel and Marilyn Leask

These Practical Guides have been designed as companions to the subject-based textbook series **Learning to Teach [Subject] in the Secondary School**. For further information on the Routledge Teaching Guides series please visit our website at www.routledge.com/education

Other titles in the series:

A Practical Guide to Teaching History in the Secondary School
Martin Hunt

A Practical Guide to Teaching Modern Foreign Languages in the Secondary School
Norbert Pachler and Ana Redondo

A Practical Guide to Teaching Citizenship in the Secondary School
Liam Gearon

A Practical Guide to Teaching ICT in the Secondary School
Steve Kennewell

A Practical Guide to Teaching Physical Education in the Secondary School

Edited by

Susan Capel, Peter Breckon and Jean O'Neill

 Routledge
Taylor & Francis Group

LONDON AND NEW YORK

First published 2006 by Routledge
2 Park Square, Milton Park, Abingdon, Oxon OX14 4RN

Simultaneously published in the USA and Canada
by Routledge
270 Madison Ave, New York, NY 10016

Routledge is an imprint of the Taylor & Francis Group, an informa business

© 2006 Susan Capel, Peter Breckon and Jean O'Neill for editorial material
and selection. Individual chapters the contributors.

Typeset in Palatino and Frutiger by
Keystroke, Jacaranda Lodge, Wolverhampton
Printed and bound in Great Britain by Bell & Bain Ltd, Glasgow

British Library Cataloguing in Publication Data
A catalogue record for this book is available from the British Library

Library of Congress Cataloging in Publication Data
A catalog record for this book has been requested

ISBN10: 0–415–36111–7
ISBN10: 0–203–00863–4 (ebk)

ISBN13: 978–0–415–36111–8
ISBN13: 978–0–203–00863–8 (ebk)

Contents

Series editors' introduction   vii
List of contributors   ix

Introduction   1

PART 1   Knowing your subject, yourself and how to make the most of learning opportunities   **3**

1   The nature of physical education   4
    MARGARET WHITEHEAD

2   How aims influence teaching   12
    MARGARET WHITEHEAD

3   The reflective practitioner   18
    PAULA ZWOZDIAK-MYERS

4   Action research   28
    PAULA ZWOZDIAK-MYERS

PART 2   Knowing your content   **39**

5   Long-term planning of the physical education curriculum   40
    PETER BRECKON AND CATHY GOWER

6   Medium- and short-term planning in physical education   50
    PETER BRECKON AND CATHY GOWER

7   Planning for pupils' learning in broader dimensions of the curriculum
    1: citizenship, social, moral, spiritual, cultural and personal development   73
    ANDY THEODOULIDES

8   Planning for pupils' learning in broader dimensions of the curriculum
    2: key skills and the use of information and communications technology   80
    RICHARD BLAIR

CONTENTS

PART 3 Teaching lessons   **89**

 9 Creating an effective learning environment which promotes 'behaviour for
    learning'   90
    SUSAN CAPEL AND JULIA LAWRENCE

10 Safe practice, risk assessment and risk management   100
    ANNE CHAPPELL

11 Maximising the achievement of all pupils   119
    JEAN O'NEILL AND KAREN PACK

12 Assessing pupils' learning   133
    JEAN O'NEILL AND DANNY OCKMORE

PART 4 Moving on   **145**

13 Working with others   146
    JEAN O'NEILL AND KAREN PACK

    Bibliography   156
    Useful websites   160
    Subject index   162
    Author index   165

Series Editors' Introduction

This practical workbook is part of a series of textbooks for student teachers. It complements and extends the popular textbook entitled *Learning to Teach in the Secondary School: A Companion to School Experience*, as well as the subject-specific textbook *Learning to Teach Physical Education in the Secondary School*. We anticipate that you will want to use this book in conjunction with these other books.

Teaching is rapidly becoming a more research- and evidence-informed profession. We have used research and professional evidence about what makes good practice to underpin the 'Learning to Teach in the Secondary School' series and these practical workbooks. Both the generic and the subject-specific books in the series provide theoretical, research and professional evidence-based advice and guidance to support you as you focus on developing aspects of your teaching or your pupils' learning as you progress through your initial teacher education course and beyond. Although the generic and subject-specific books include some case studies and tasks to help you consider the issues, the practical application of material is not their major focus. That is the role of this book.

This book aims to reinforce your understanding of aspects of your teaching, support you in aspects of your development as a teacher and your teaching and enable you to analyse your success as a teacher in maximising pupils' learning by focusing on practical applications. The practical activities in this book can be used in a number of ways. Some activities are designed to be undertaken by you individually, others as a joint task in pairs and yet others as group work working with, for example, other student teachers or a school- or university-based tutor. Your tutor may use the activities with a group of student teachers. The book has been designed so that you can write directly into it.

In England, new ways of working for teachers are being developed through an initiative remodelling the school workforce. This may mean that you have a range of colleagues to support in your classroom. They also provide an additional resource on which you can draw. In any case, you will, of course, need to draw on additional resources to support your development and the *Learning to Teach in the Secondary School, 4th edition* website (http://www.routledge.com/textbooks/0415363926) lists key websites for Scotland, Wales, Northern Ireland and England. For example, key websites relevant to teachers in England include the Teacher Training Resource Bank (www.ttrb.ac.uk). Others include: www.teachernet.gov.uk. which is part of the DfES schools web initiative; www.becta.org.uk, which has ICT resources; and www.qca.org.uk. which is the Qualifications and Curriculum Authority website.

We do hope that this practical workbook will be useful in supporting your development as a teacher.

Susan Capel
Marilyn Leask
January 2006

Contributors

Richard Blair is a physical education teacher.

Peter Breckon is subject leader for physical education and course leader for the BSc secondary physical education degree at Brunel University.

Susan Capel is a professor in the School of Sport and Education at Brunel University.

Anne Chappell is a lecturer in physical education at Brunel University.

Cathy Gower is a lecturer in physical education at Brunel University, with specific responsibility for running the PGCE secondary physical education course.

Julia Lawrence is a lecturer in the School of Sport and Education at Brunel University.

Danny Ockmore leads the physical education department at Claverham Community College in East Sussex.

Jean O'Neill lectures in physical education and is the school partnership coordinator at the Chelsea School, University of Brighton.

Karen Pack is Director of Specialism at the Coopers Company at Coborn School in Upminster, Essex.

Andy Theodoulides lectures in physical education and is course leader for the PGCE secondary physical education course at the Chelsea School, University of Brighton.

Margaret Whitehead is a physical education consultant.

Paula Zwozdiak-Myers lectures in physical education at De Montfort University, Bedford, where she is head of professional studies for the secondary degree programme in physical education.

Introduction

This workbook covers the practical application of a range of topics particularly relevant to physical education. It has been specifically written to be used alongside the textbook, *Learning to Teach Physical Education in the Secondary School: A Companion to School Experience*, but could equally be used on its own.

The book addresses:

- what physical education is and what its aims are;
- your development as a teacher – including the development of knowledge to become a reflective practitioner;
- long-, medium- and short-term planning – including incorporating broader aspects of pupils' learning in your teaching;
- aspects of teaching your lessons, including safety, promoting positive pupil behaviour, maximising pupil achievement and assessment of pupils;
- working with others outside your classroom.

Each chapter includes:

- an introduction, setting out the aims and rationale of the chapter;
- some background information about the specific topic, the research base or professional insights from classroom observations and experience. This is supported by a range of practical activities, including some of the following:

  - case studies or scenarios;
  - lesson plans/evaluations;
  - worksheets;
  - reflections on hypothetical, observed or taught lessons;
  - planning how to use material in your teaching;
  - setting a learning activity for pupils;
  - reflective questions;
  - personal audit

- further readings and/or links that provide an in-depth reading to supplement the material in this text.

Different terminology is adopted on different Initial Teacher Education (ITE) courses. The terminology used in this book might not be the same as that used in your particular ITE situation. One area in which terminology differs is the use of the terms 'objectives' and 'learning outcomes'. In Chapters 1 and 2 you are asked to consider both terms. On some courses the term 'objectives' is used to identify what pupils will be able to do both at the end of the unit of work and the lesson plan; on other courses, the term 'objectives' is used to identify what pupils will be able to do at the end of the unit of work and the term 'learning outcomes' (sometimes with a word such as 'intended' added) is used to identify what pupils will be able to do at the end of a lesson; on other courses, the term 'learning outcomes' is used to identify what pupils will be able to do at both the end of a unit of work and a lesson. (Sometimes both terms are used in units of work and the lesson plan, e.g. the QCA units use both 'learning objectives' and 'learning outcomes' in their units of work.) Chapter 6 gives an example of where the term 'intended learning outcomes' is used for both units of work and lesson plans. The term 'learning outcomes' is used in the rest of the book to identify what pupils will be able to do at the end of a lesson.

Likewise, different practices are adopted on different ITE courses. One particular example of different practices is different formats for unit of work and lesson planning. These illustrate different ways of presenting the same information. They may also be different to the formats you use on your ITE course. We suggest you use these as examples of different ways in which similar information may be presented, then select the format most appropriate for your needs.

Further, different ITE courses use different means of achieving the same end. For example, on some courses lesson learning outcomes are written for the whole class, and achievement of pupils against the learning outcomes forms part of the formative and summative assessment. However, on other courses, it is the learning outcomes themselves that are differentiated to cater for the range of pupils in the class. For example, learning outcomes can be divided into three bands: those that can be achieved by most of the pupils in the class, with different learning outcomes for pupils who cannot achieve those and additional outcomes for those pupils who need to be extended further. This use of terminology is shown in Chapter 12.

We hope that this practical workbook will be useful in supporting your development as a teacher. The book has been designed so that you can write directly into it and therefore keep it as a record of your work. Some proformas and further resources are available on the companion website at http://www.routledge.com/textbooks/0415361117

Part 1 Knowing your subject, yourself and how to make the most of learning opportunities

Chapter 1 The nature of physical education

MARGARET WHITEHEAD

INTRODUCTION

This chapter is designed to help you to clarify your thinking about key aspects of the nature of physical education. It looks at the relationship between aims, objectives and learning outcomes and how aims relate to values and justifications. It also encourages you to think about the difference between physical education and related activities such as sport, as well as alert you to the way aims can be ends in themselves or means to other ends. In essence, this chapter has a philosophical flavour and rather than give you all the answers, it challenges you to reflect on your current thinking and to appreciate that there will always be different opinions about many of the important issues covered here.

By the end of this chapter you should be able to:

*   employ the terms 'aim', 'objective' and 'learning outcome' accurately;
*   identify the relationship between an 'aim', a 'value' and a 'justification';
*   differentiate between key concepts in physical education and sport;
*   recognise aims that are ends in themselves and those that are means to other ends.

AIMS, OBJECTIVES AND LEARNING OUTCOMES

It is very important to be clear about the aims underlying physical education and how these relate to units of work and lesson planning. Aims are usually defined as long-term intentions of a subject. The stepping stones to achieve an aim are usually referred to as objectives and are the intentions that guide the planning of units of work. Steps to achieve objectives are usually referred to as learning outcomes and these are written in such a way to describe specifically what pupils are able to demonstrate (see also Whitehead, 2004).

Complete Activity 1.1a. This allows you to check that you have grasped both the relationship between these three important terms and the difference between these concepts.

AIMS, VALUE AND JUSTIFICATIONS

The previous section looked at aims and how these are broken down in stages and thus impact on the actual nature of the teaching of pupils. The other important aspect of aims is their role in justifying the place of the subject in the curriculum. Rather than putting aims under the microscope as in the section above, this consideration of aims looks outwards at how the subject relates to education as a whole and the place of physical activity in society. It is very important for all teachers of physical education to be able to articulate the value of the aims of the subject and be able to support this value claim with a justification.

Activity 1.1a Aims, objectives and learning outcomes

From the list below, identify which is an aim, which is an objective, which is a learning outcome value and which is a justification:

- Introduce pair work in simple sports acrobatic balances
- Show stability in holding a pair balance
- Develop the body management skill of balancing

Complete the steps below by adding an objective and a learning outcome:

- Aim – develop co-operative skills
- Objective
- Learning outcome

Complete the steps below by adding an aim and a learning outcome:

- Aim
- Objective – introduce 5 vs 5 game of hockey
- Learning outcome

Complete the steps below by adding an aim and an objective

- Aim
- Objective
- Learning outcome – be able to record the heart rate before and after activity

Aims are statements of your intended goals. They answer the question, 'Why are you carrying out this practice?' *Values* answer the question, 'What is the point of carrying out this practice?' In other words, a value describes the benefit to be gained from a particular activity. A *justification* responds to the next question, 'Can you persuade me that the value you attribute to the practice is worthwhile?' A justification, therefore goes a step further and explains why the claimed benefit is desirable. There is further discussion of these concepts in Whitehead (2004).

For example, one could be asked, 'Why are you catching this train?' The answer could be 'To go to London.' The value question would be, 'What are you going to London for?' The answer could be 'To do Christmas shopping.' The justification question following this could be, 'What is the advantage of going to London if you could do all your shopping in Sheffield?' Your answer could indicate the amount of choice in London or that the prices are cheaper.

Similar questions in relation to physical education could be:

- Why are you doing physical education? Answer: to promote skilful body management.
- What is the value of promoting skilful body management? Answer: to help pupils to be co-ordinated and be able to control their body.
- Why is this a valuable thing to do? Answer: as humans we need to be able to function effectively physically not only to carry out activities in our daily life with ease but also to give us the opportunity to take part in the wide range of physical activities available in our culture.

Complete Activity 1.1b to check that you have grasped the relationship between an aim, a value and a justification and appreciate the distinctive nature of each concept.

Activity 1.1b   Aims, values and justifications

From the list below, identify which is an aim, which is a value and which is a justification:

- Competition is an integral part of our culture
- Learn to handle competition
- To experience and manage winning and losing

Complete the trio below by adding the value and justification:

- Aim – to develop physical literacy
- Value
- Justification

Complete the trio below by adding the aim and justification:

- Aim
- Value – to ensure lifelong health and fitness
- Justification

Complete the trio below by adding the aim and value:

- Aim
- Value
- Justification – imagination and creativity are integral aspects of life and offer the potential to enrich many aspects of work and leisure

---

DEFINING TERMS SUCH AS PHYSICAL EDUCATION AND SPORT

One complication in debating aims, values and justifications is that there could be an underlying misunderstanding about the subject under debate. For example, some people find it difficult to differentiate between physical education and sport; others see both physical education and sport as forms of recreation. How people understand the meaning of a term influences their view of its value. For example, if people think that physical education is simply recreation, they may see no justification for it to be taught in school. If people believe that physical education is simply a vehicle for teaching competitive team games, they will question attention being given to dance in the curriculum. For these reasons, you need to be clear about the meanings of different terms. While everyone else may not agree with you, you need to know and be able to state what you understand by a particular term.

The way terms are used is often differentiated by the following:

- who is taking part;
- what activities are being undertaken;
- where the activity is occurring;
- why the participants are taking part;
- what the purpose of the activity is;

- what the participants are wearing;
- whether participants have to pay to take part.

Use Activities 1.2a and 1.2b to answer these questions in relation to a range of terms.

Activity 1.2a

Concept	Who is taking part?	What activities are being undertaken?	Where is it occurring?
Physical Education			
Movement Education			
School Sport			
Extra-curricular activity			
Sport			
Leisure			
Recreation			

Activity 1.2b

Concept	Why are people taking part? (Optional, compulsory, cultural)	What is the purpose of the activity?	What are people wearing and have they had to pay to take part?
Physical Education			
Movement Education			
School Sport			
Extra-curricular activity			
Sport			
Leisure			
Recreation			

From your answers, create a definition for each of the terms given. As well as discussing with another student teacher or your mentor, it could also be useful to discuss your definitions with someone outside the world of physical education and sport. Having completed this exercise, look up in a range of literature how others have defined these terms and compare these with your thoughts. You can find definitions in numerous publications such as Department for Education and Employment/Qualifications and Curriculum Authority (DfEE/QCA, 1999) and Department of Education and Science (DES, 1991).

It is important to remember that there will never be one specific definition. However, it is critical that you know to what you are referring and can recognise if there are misunderstandings between people.

AIMS OF PHYSICAL EDUCATION: AS ENDS IN THEMSELVES OR MEANS TO OTHER ENDS?

It is important to recognise that there are two types of aims: first, those which are unique to physical education, intrinsic to the subject and see physical education as an end in itself; and, second, those which the subject shares with other aspects of the curriculum, are extrinsic to physical education and use the subject as a means to broader educational goals.

An example of performing an action as an end in itself or as a means to other ends can be given in relation to eating food. One can eat food simply to provide enough energy and nutriment to support your daily lifestyle. In this case, eating is an end in itself. However, if you eat particular foods either to build muscle or stamina or simply for pleasure, the action has an extrinsic purpose beyond enabling you to live your habitual lifestyle. Other actions could also help you to realise these ends. For example, weight training would support muscle development and watching a film could give pleasure.

In the context of physical education, we might claim that the subject promotes language development. This is clearly using physical education as a means to extrinsic ends; certainly ends that can be achieved by other subject areas.

Activity 1.3a Aims of physical education as ends in themselves or means to other ends

From the list below, identify which aims can be categorised clearly as *ends* for physical education itself, those which are clearly using physical education as a *means* to achieve broader educational goals and those where there might be some *debate* as to whether they are ends- or means-related.

Physical education aims to enable pupils to do the following:

- take initiative
- develop their own ideas in a creative way
- become skilful and intelligent performers
- gain knowledge and understanding of fitness and health
- refrain from anti-social behaviour
- develop self-confidence and self-esteem
- develop skilful body management
- take part effectively in a range of team games
- develop perseverance
- develop positive attitudes to learning
- develop a range of thinking skills
- handle competition effectively
- realise the potential range and scope of their bodily abilities
- make judgements about their own ability and progress.

Complete Activity 1.3a to check that you recognise which aims of physical education are ends in themselves and which are means to other ends. It will not be surprising if you are uncertain about the exact nature of each aim listed.

In relation to considering physical education as an end in itself and a means to other ends, an approach that is often taken is to consider the notions of education *in* movement, education *about* movement and education *through* movement (see Arnold, 1988, for definitions of these terms). Complete the task in activity 1.3b.

Activity 1.3b Education in, through and about movement

Read Arnold (1988, pp. 106–14) and list below activities and approaches to physical education that he identifies as in, through and about movement.

- Education *in* movement

- Education *through* movement

- Education *about* movement

How far do you find this differentiation acceptable and helpful?

SUMMARY

The aim of this chapter was to help you to understand the relationship between aims, objectives and learning outcomes and between aims, values and justifications. A sound grasp of the first relationship is essential in all aspects of planning, while your ability to argue cogently in support of the values and justifications of physical education will be important throughout your career. Your ability to put the case for physical education will be enhanced if you are clear both about the nature of the terms you are using, and the difference between aims that are ends in themselves and means to other ends. While there is a broad consensus about many of these topics, there will always be a variety of opinions and it is very important that you begin to think through where you stand on these much debated issues.

FURTHER READING

Whitehead, M. (2000) Aims as an issue in physical education, in S. Capel and S. Piotrowski (eds) *Issues in Physical Education*, London: RoutledgeFalmer, pp. 7–21. This chapter addresses a range of issues in respect of the aims of physical education including the notion of aims as ends in themselves and as means to other ends. There is a brief consideration of the debates surrounding the tensions between promoting excellence or advocating inclusion, and between seeing the process of teaching/learning in physical education as of more significance than the product. In addition, the chapter looks briefly at curricular implications of adopting certain extrinsic aims.

Whitehead, M. (2004) Aims of PE, in S. Capel (ed.) *Learning to Teach Physical Education in the Secondary School: A Companion to School Experience*, 2nd edn, London: RoutledgeFalmer, pp. 17–26. This chapter discusses the aims of physical education in the broader context of the aims of education and looks at the range of aims that have been claimed for the subject. In addition, there is further discussion of aims, values and justifications and of aims as ends in themselves and as means to other ends.

For articles on physical literacy, see the website www.physical-literacy.org.uk

Chapter 2 How aims influence teaching

MARGARET WHITEHEAD

INTRODUCTION

The predominant focus of Chapter 1 was to help you to be clear about the nature of aims, objectives and learning outcomes and to understand the relationship between aims, values and justifications. This chapter focuses on one very important aspect of aims and objectives; their relationship to planning lessons both with respect to the material to be covered and the teaching approaches you might employ (see Chapter 6). Aims, objectives and learning outcomes are also key issues in the areas of assessment and evaluation (see Chapter 12).

It is important for you to realise that while physical education has the potential to realise a wide range of goals, the achievement of these depends wholly on your selection of appropriate content and teaching approaches. Aims such as developing communication skills will not be achieved automatically through pupil involvement in physical education. The selection of content and teaching method is critical to the achievement of aims and objectives. For example, if an objective of a physical education unit of work is to develop creativity, the lesson content and teaching approaches must be planned to allow pupils sufficient freedom to take decisions themselves. If an aim of the subject is to give pupils experience of a wide and varied range of physical activities, a curriculum comprised wholly of team games will not realise this goal.

By the end of this chapter you should be able to:

- identify content appropriate to realising aims/objectives;
- identify teaching approaches conducive to realising aims/objectives;
- identify the qualities needed for the teacher as a professional;
- recognise personal strengths and areas to be developed in yourself.

Before you read any further, we suggest that you read Chapters 8 and 9 and Whitehead with Zwozdiak-Myers (2004) and Zwozdiak-Myers *et al.* (2004) which cover the overall relationship between aims and teaching.

AIMS/OBJECTIVES AND CONTENT

Activity 2.1 lists a range of aims/objectives both of physical education as an end in itself and of physical education as a means to achieving other ends such as those related to key skills, thinking skills and the development of citizenship.

Complete the right-hand column of this sheet indicating which activities/aspects of activities could provide a framework for the aim/objective to be achieved. For example, if an aim was to help pupils appreciate the value of physical activity to becoming healthy, the

Activity 2.1

Aim/objective	Content to achieve aim/objective alongside each aim suggest a number of activities/aspects of activities through which it could be achieved
Aims/objectives in which physical education is an end in itself • Developing body control, co-ordination and balance • Relating effectively through movement with others, missiles and objects in the environment • Developing strength • Experiencing the aesthetic aspects of movement	
Key skills and thinking skills • Communicating • Making judgements • Problem solving • Reasoning • Grasping whole/part relationships	
Characteristics related to citizenship • Applying and respecting rules e.g. competitive team games • Developing loyalty • Understanding other cultures • Working co-operatively	

type of content might include, for example, health-related fitness activities, swimming, athletics, circuit training and possibly some lessons that have a more theoretical approach.

AIMS/OBJECTIVES AND TEACHING APPROACHES

Activity 2.2a lists a range of aims/objectives of physical education, again, both those that are ends in themselves and those that are means to other ends. For each aim/objective suggest how you need to conduct a lesson to achieve each aim. The suggestions could be broad or very specific. For example, if the aim was to develop creativity, a broad example could indicate that time should be set aside in the lesson for pupils to explore ideas for themselves rather than be directed by the teacher. A very specific example could be that the teacher should look to praise individuals for innovative ideas.

Activity 2.2a Teaching approaches to achieve aims/objectives

Against each aim/objective listed identify constituents of teaching and teaching approaches, the use of which could aid pupil achievement.

- Develop physical skills.

- Become an intelligent performer.

- Select compositional ideas, e.g. set a specific task in Dance to create a group composition.

- Evaluate own performance.

- Understand fitness and health.

- Take initiative.

- Develop positive attitudes to participation in physical activity.

- Handle competition appropriately.

- Take responsibility.

- Develop co-operative skills.

- Develop self-confidence and self-esteem.

Activity 2.2b asks you to start from the 'other end' and consider when it would be appropriate for a teacher to use certain approaches. For example, it would be appropriate for the teacher to use peer teaching if the intention is to begin to develop co-operative skills.

Activity 2.2b Appropriate use of aspects of teaching to achieve aims/objectives

Against each aspect of teaching/teaching approach below suggest the aim/objective to which you might be working if you employed such an element in your teaching.

- A series of work cards of increasing challenge.

- Recall questions, e.g. at the start of a lesson to remind pupils of the work of the previous lesson and to help them to understand the work you have covered.

- Use of visual aids on a work area wall.

- Feedback highlighting effort.

- Highly directed practices.

- Devolution of assessment of self to each pupil.

- Peer teaching.

- Pupils recording outcomes on paper.

- Grouping decided by the teacher.

- Problem-solving tasks.

- A series of short varied practices.

- Pupil demonstration.

THE TEACHER AS A PROFESSIONAL

Chapters 1 and 2 have set out a range of broad principles underpinning your work as a physical education teacher, for example, the key role of aims, the need to be able to articulate the value of the subject and the relationship between aims and objectives and how you plan and structure your teaching. A grasp of these principles is very important as you develop all aspects of your teaching. The next section of the chapter asks you to reflect broadly on the nature of teaching and the skills and qualities needed by all teachers, by physical education teachers and, finally, but most importantly, to reflect on how far, to date, you have mastered these skills and acquired these qualities.

In Activity 2.3, part (a) asks you to list the qualities needed by teachers and then specifically by physical education teachers; part (b) asks you to carry out some self-reflection on your current strengths as a teacher and challenges you to map out some goals for the future. You may want to return to this sheet on a number of occasions. Part (c) challenges you to consider where your priorities lie in relation to the aims of physical education. Again, you may want to return to this task on a number of occasions. It will not be unusual if your priorities change during your training.

Activity 2.3

(a) Teacher as a Professional 1

- List the qualities needed in *all* teachers, e.g. patience.
- List the qualities needed in *physical education* teachers.

Compare the similarities and differences in the two lists.

(b) Teacher as a Professional 2

Self-analysis. From the lists above, identify:

- aspects of your teaching that are strengths;
- aspects of your teaching that need attention.

How are you going to develop these? Identify your preferred teaching approaches and select other approaches that may need to be developed.

(c) Teacher as a Professional 3

Developing your own philosophy about what is important in physical education. From the variety of aims of physical education identified in Chapter 1 select two aims where physical education is an end in itself and two aims where physical education is a means to another end. State the value of each aim selected and support the importance of each value by identifying its justification.

- Aim 1
- Aim 2
- Aim 3
- Aim 4

There is a proforma on the website (http://www.routledge.com/textbooks/0415361117) that you may want to use to help you undertake this activity.

SUMMARY

This chapter has set tasks to help you to understand the relationship between aims and objectives and the lesson content and teaching approaches used with the pupils. This link between intentions and planning and teaching is absolutely critical, as unless teaching is specifically designed to achieve an intended outcome, that goal is very unlikely to be realised. The chapter also asked you to consider the nature of the teacher as a professional and the particular characteristics needed by physical education teachers. An understanding of these issues was used to form a background for you to consider your strengths as a teacher and areas in which you still need to work. The final task challenged you to begin to formulate your own philosophy of physical education by asking you to list where your priorities lie in respect of aims for the subject.

FURTHER READING

Leah, J. and Capel, S. (2000) Competition and co-operation in physical education, in S. Capel and S. Piotrowski (eds) *Issues in Physical Education*, London: RoutledgeFalmer, pp. 144–58. This is a useful chapter that looks at the implications of using two particular approaches to teaching.

Leask, M. (2005) Becoming a teacher, in S. Capel, S., M. Leask and T. Turner (eds) *Learning to Teach in the Secondary School: A Companion to School Experience*, 4th edn, London: RoutledgeFalmer, pp. 5–6 and Further Reading texts. A useful short section looking at the issue of what it means to be a professional.

Mosston, M. and Ashworth, S. (2002) *Teaching Physical Education*, 5th edn, San Francisco: Benjamin Cummings. This is a valuable text looking at approaches to teaching with particular reference to the objectives that can be achieved through using these different teaching methods.

Chapter 3 — The reflective practitioner

PAULA ZWOZDIAK-MYERS

INTRODUCTION

One very important aspect of teaching and learning about teaching involves the process of reflection and this chapter aims to develop your understanding of, and capacity for, reflection.

By the end of this chapter you should be able to:

- understand how reflection might be conceptualised;
- know where in teaching reflection should take place;
- know how to engage in reflective practice;
- understand why reflecting on your practice is important.

UNDERSTAND HOW REFLECTION MIGHT BE CONCEPTUALISED

Reflection has been described by Loughran (1996: 14) as 'the deliberate and purposeful act of thinking which centres on ways of responding to problem situations in teaching and learning'. This view of the way teachers think about their practice involves a number of steps or phases in thinking which, when organised and linked, lead to a consequence in action.

In his model of reflective thought Dewey (1933) identified five phases or states of thinking: *suggestions*, *problem*, *hypothesis*, *reasoning* and *testing*. Each phase is contextualised by past and future actions and experiences and some might be expanded or overlap, depending on the nature of the problem. Although these phases need not necessarily link in any particular order, when pieced together, they form a process of *reflective thinking* that involves: '(1) a state of doubt, hesitation, perplexity, mental difficulty, in which thinking originates, and (2) an act of searching, hunting, inquiring, to find material that will resolve the doubt, settle and dispose of the perplexity' (ibid.:12).

Dewey considered that attitudes of *open-mindedness*, *whole-heartedness* and *responsibility* were important in the use of reflection. Boud *et al.* (1985: 19) consider reflection to be an activity in which people 'recapture their experience, think about it, mull it over and evaluate it'. They include the dimension of feelings and emotions in their interpretation of reflection and reconfigure Dewey's five phases into three: *returning to experience*, *attending to (or connecting with) feelings*, and *evaluating experience*.

The importance of reflecting on what you are doing, as part of the learning process, has been emphasised by many educational theorists. Schön (1983) built on and extended Dewey's work on the properties of reflection and suggested that the capacity to reflect on action so as to engage in a process of continuous learning is one of the defining characteristics of professional practice. A new wave of research and learning about reflection emerged in the mid-1980s in response to Schön's concept of reflection as 'knowledge gained from the practitioner's own experience' through 'reconstructing experience'. It therefore takes place in the 'crucible of action' (Grimmett and Erickson, 1988: 13).

Schön distinguished between two fundamental processes: reflection *in* action and reflection *on* action:

1   *Reflection in action* (while doing something) is understood through such phrases as *thinking on your feet and keeping your wits about you* which suggest that 'not only can we think about doing but that we can think about doing something whilst doing it. Some of the most interesting examples of this process occur in the midst of performance' (Schön, 1983: 54).

2   *Reflection on action* (after you have done something), similar to Dewey's notion of reflection, is the basis of much literature that is related to reflective teaching and reflective teacher education. This form of reflection is seen as 'the systematic and deliberate thinking back over one's actions . . . [it involves] . . . teachers who are thoughtful about their work' (Russell and Munby, 1992: 3). The insights gained about aspects of teaching and learning about teaching are subsequently used to inform future practice.

Now complete Activity 3.1.

Activity 3.1   How reflection might be conceptualised

Conduct a web-based search to further elaborate the contributions of Dewey (1933), Boud *et al.* (1985) and Schön (1983) on 'how reflection might be conceptualised' using the following sites: http://www.infed.org/biblio/b-reflect.htm; http://www.infed.org/thinkers/et-schon.htm

---

KNOW WHERE IN TEACHING REFLECTION SHOULD TAKE PLACE

Situations where reflection, in teaching and learning about teaching, should occur to inform your practice include:

- reflection in action;
- reflection on action;
- reflection on your teaching as a whole.

Reflection in action

Reflection in action takes place within the context of an ongoing lesson and involves monitoring the class by observing pupils as they work, on given tasks in a specific situation and environment, to judge whether the intended learning outcomes are being achieved. Having observed pupil response, you must then decide what action needs to be taken to maximise learning opportunities in the lesson. Some of these actions will be minor modifications to your plan whereas others might require a more substantial review. In both instances, you must respond to the class to guide the work towards their learning the intended learning outcomes.

Due to the transient nature of the teaching-learning context, when situations arise that could either inhibit or promote pupils' knowledge and understanding of concepts and skills you should, whenever possible, respond to them as soon as they occur. This relates directly to the development of your observation skills and ability to 'read the class' along with your ability to draw from your repertoire of relevant past experiences and of your personal frame of reference. Activity 3.2a asks you to think about reflection in action.

Activity 3.2a   Reflection in action

Complete the table below by identifying what action(s) you might take *during the lesson* as a consequence of observing the following pupil responses. Add some exemplars from your own experience.

Pupil response	Action(s) you might take	Why is this action being taken?
• Some group work is of very high quality	e.g. extension tasks are set	To ensure all are working at their own ability
• Confused by task		
• Inattentive		
• Pairs working through progressions at different rates		
• One pupil being physically bullied		
• Chatty group is off-task		
• Some individuals appear disinterested		
• Whether pupil/s for whom English is an additional language (EAL) respond to a given task appropriately		
•		
•		
•		
•		

Reflection on action

Reflection on action is usually undertaken once you have taught a lesson or a series of lessons (end of unit of work). This enables you to judge, for example, what was happening with a particular group of pupils in a particular teaching situation and to explore how and why you acted as you did.

Post lesson

This reflection involves looking back at what happened during a lesson, considering why things (e.g. the poor level of behaviour) occurred. Such questions should be responded to on your lesson evaluation as soon as possible after the lesson. Although the focus for this reflection may be on the teaching, you should begin the process by identifying what proportion of pupils achieved each of the lesson learning outcomes. Based upon this evidence, you must consider your influence on this learning or lack of learning, and question the outcome. For example, if all pupils achieved a particular learning outcome you might question whether it was appropriate for their level of ability or, if some did not achieve a particular learning outcome you should question why they did not succeed. You should also evaluate the overall quality of the lesson including the introduction, transitions and plenary.

Responses to *why* (the questions raised) are vital aspects of your reflection and self-appraisal since they guide your thinking on *how* to plan the next lesson to ensure that pupils achieve the next set of learning outcomes. Successful approaches that you have identified should be revisited and less successful aspects changed. These aspects, both successful and less successful, may become your teacher performance targets when teaching your next lesson.

Post unit of work

A similar process to that described above should be undertaken at the end of each unit of work, when you evaluate how far you have achieved the unit outcomes. This reflection should provide insight of both your pupils' future developmental needs, and your personal development in terms of the knowledge, skills and understanding required to effectively accommodate these. This reflection could influence how you teach the class in question in their next unit and/or how you teach this unit to another class. Activity 3.2b asks you to think about reflection on action.

Reflection on the development of your teaching as a whole

During each school experience you receive a considerable amount of verbal, visual and written feedback that focuses on different aspects of your development as a teacher. For example, you receive valuable feedback from your pupils during a question/answer session to ascertain whether they have understood a particular skill or concept and you receive focused lesson observation critiques from your tutor. You are also required to evaluate each of your lessons/units of work and to undertake a range of school-based tasks.

From this emerging 'evidence' base you must consider the effectiveness of your teaching in the interests of all your pupils' learning. This can be quite a challenging exercise to engage in during the early stages of your school experience. For example, at the beginning it might have been pointed out to you that, for example, you were disorganised in your classroom management and organisation, or that you did not use demonstration to introduce new skills and concepts to best advantage. It is in the interests of all your pupils for you to work on improving these particular aspects of your teaching.

Reflection on the development of your teaching as a whole means that you take into account the 'whole picture'; you analyse the effectiveness of a lesson or series of lessons in order to evaluate 'what was learned, by whom, and how more effective learning might take

Activity 3.2b Reflection on action

In relation to aspects of your teaching, identify possible reasons why opportunities for pupil learning might be *maximised* or *inhibited*. Draw on personal experience where possible. How can you transform the inhibited learning opportunities into maximised ones?

Aspect of teaching	Maximised pupil learning opportunities	Inhibited pupil learning opportunities
Planning, expectations and targets	• e.g. conditioned game for more able • • •	• e.g. unrealistic targets for many pupils • • •
Class management and organisation	• e.g. matched ability groups • • •	• e.g. poor behaviour ignored • • •
Strategy/tasks	• e.g. focused questions • • •	• e.g. limited feedback • • •
Content knowledge	• e.g. new concepts build on prior knowledge/skills • • •	• e.g. inaccurate technique demonstrated • • •

place in the future' (Moore, 2000: 129). This involves a systematic analysis of your current practice by careful evaluation of your own 'classroom performance, planning and assessment, in conjunction with evaluations of students' behaviour and achievement' (ibid.: 129). This also requires an understanding of relevant educational theory and research, for example, theories of cognitive development and pupils' preferred learning styles, when coming to understand issues that are not only concerned with the 'what' and 'when' of education but moreover, embrace the questions of 'how' and 'why'.

The times when you might be asked to reflect on your teaching as a whole include:

- Regular debriefing sessions with your tutor when weekly targets should be set in consultation with your tutor and your reflection of achievements of these should provide the content of your weekly evaluation.
- At the end of each school experience placement, you should identify targets for your next school placement with your tutor.
- Regular points during your degree course with your personal tutor to identify targets for your continuing professional development.

For each occasion, you should generate a list of targets or next steps – each of which is the outcome of reflecting on the development of your teaching as a whole. The focus for these targets will be directly linked to specific assessment criteria that are used to identify effective teaching and the standards you need to achieve to qualify as a teacher. These standards provide the syllabus that you, as a developing teacher, will work through systematically and progressively until the completion of your initial teacher education. Activity 3.2c makes you reflect on your teaching as a whole.

KNOW HOW TO ENGAGE IN REFLECTIVE PRACTICE

Informed by your readings of 'how reflection might be conceptualised' along with an increased awareness of 'where in teaching reflection should take place' you have come, in part, to realise 'how to engage in reflective practice'. This process begins after you have taught your very first lesson and seek to answer the question 'Did it go well?' In reviewing the effectiveness of your teaching, Kyriacou (1998: 124) suggests that two key aspects of appraisal need to be considered: 'First, what aspects of your teaching need to be considered in order to improve your future practice?' and 'Second, how can you best go about improving your practice in the area that could usefully be developed?' Activity 3.3 shows you how to engage in reflective practice.

UNDERSTAND WHY REFLECTING ON YOUR PRACTICE IS IMPORTANT

The purpose, rationale and justification for all of this reflection is to improve the effectiveness of your teaching in order to maximise the learning opportunities that you provide for pupils.

All three types of reflection – in action, on action and on your teaching as a whole – should be developed since they are an integral part of a teacher's way of life and should continue to be a part of your practice throughout your teaching career. Activity 3.4 helps you to understand why reflecting on your practice is important.

Activity 3.2c   Reflection on your teaching as a whole

Identify in relation to each of the Standards (given to you by your institution or at http://www.tta.gov.uk), and using the format below for planning, teaching and assessment: (1) problems you encountered and resolved, and (2) problems you encountered but could not resolve, during your most recent school experience.

Aspect of teaching	Problem	Solution – resolved
Planning	e.g. learning outcomes not specific	Worked with mentor on writing specific learning outcomes, focusing on the use of verb, language context and quality (see Chapter 6)
Teaching		
Assessment		

Aspect of teaching	Problem	Unresolved
Planning		
Teaching		
Assessment		

- What alternative strategies are there to the resolved problems? What possible solutions are there to the unresolved problems?
- How did you arrive at the solutions?
- What knowledge and skills did you need?
- What thinking and decision-making processes did you go through?

Activity 3.3 How to engage in reflective practice

Using the chart below, identify from Activity 3.2c:

1   which aspects of your teaching need to be considered in order to improve your
       future practice (organise them under appropriate headings in column 1)

Then complete the remaining columns in relation to:

2   strategies you could use to improve these aspects of your teaching;
3   how and when you could put these into action;
4   what criteria you would use to judge how well the strategies worked;
5   where you can expect to find evidence to support your judgements.

Try these out and appraise their impact so as to inform future practice

1 Aspect of teaching	2 Strategies	3 How	4 When	5 Criteria	6 Where

Activity 3.4 Why reflecting on your practice is important

Look back over your evaluations for three lessons that you have taught recently. In relation to aspects of your teaching that need further development record what you plan to do, how you plan to do it and why this is important.

What you plan to do	How you plan to do it	Why this is important
Lesson 1: 1 2 3		
Lesson 2: 1 2 3		
Lesson 3: 1 2 3		

- Identify five consequences that should emerge from systematically reflecting on aspects of your teaching and learning about teaching.
- Identify five consequences that might emerge from failing to systematically reflect on aspects of your teaching and learning about teaching.
- Compare both sets of consequences to enable you to make change where appropriate.

SUMMARY

We hope that this chapter has provided you with the basis for developing your skills of reflection. In order to help you further, Chapter 4 looks at action research. This encourages teachers to engage in the process of systematic critical reflection about their own current practice so as to move in an informed and principled way towards developing mastery of their chosen craft.

ACKNOWLEDGEMENT

Some ideas for the approach used in this chapter arose from work by Margaret Whitehead.

FURTHER READING

Kyriacou, C. (1998) *Essential Teaching Skills*, 2nd edn, London: Stanley Thornes
Moore, A. (2000) *Teaching and Learning, Pedagogy, Curriculum and Culture*, London: RoutledgeFalmer

Chapter 4   Action research

PAULA ZWOZDIAK-MYERS

INTRODUCTION

This chapter is designed to develop your understanding of the principles of action research and to recognise its potential within the teaching-learning context. By the end of this chapter you should be able to:

- understand how action research might be conceptualised;
- know how to identify a focus for action research;
- know how to engage in the action research process.

UNDERSTAND HOW ACTION RESEARCH MIGHT BE CONCEPTUALISED

When teachers ask searching questions of their own educational practice they exemplify a commitment to continuous learning by seeking new ideas, evaluating and reflecting on their impact and trying out new practices and ways of working to improve their own effectiveness in the teaching-learning environment (Hargreaves *et al.*, 2001). 'The ultimate aim of inquiry is understanding; and understanding is the basis of action for improvement' (McKernan, 1996: 3).

Action research is a 'particularly valuable way for teachers to evaluate and critique their own current practice and to move in an informed and principled way towards more effective future practice' (Moore, 2000: 146). Carr and Kemmis (1986: 162) define action research as: 'a form of self-reflective enquiry undertaken by participants in social situations in order to improve the rationality and justice of their own practices, their understanding of these practices, and the situations in which the practices are carried out'.

Central to the concept of the teacher as researcher is the 'systematic reflection on one's classroom experience, to understand it and to create meaning out of that understanding' (Hopkins, 2002: 5). Now complete Activity 4.1a.

Ethical considerations

Before undertaking any form of research with children in school there are a number of ethical issues that must be addressed. Activity 4.1b indicates the kind of ethical considerations that should be important to you.

Activity 4.1a How action research might be conceptualised

Read Chapter 4 'Action research and classroom research by teachers' in Hopkins (2002: 42–54). Make notes on the six principles that Hopkins suggests should be followed by teachers when undertaking classroom research, stating the extent to which you feel that you understand how to proceed in relation to each principle.

If you want to pursue this further, you might also like to look at the similarities and differences between four models of action research, i.e. Kemmis (1988), Elliott (1991), Ebbutt (1985) and McKernan (1996).

Activity 4.1b Ethical considerations

Record below the ethical issues that need to be addressed *before* you undertake any form of research with children in school. See, for example, the British Educational Research Association guidelines (BERA, 2000)

- *parental permission*

-

-

-

-

-

-

Find out what documentation you need to complete for ethical approval *before* you undertake any form of research with children in school. Record these below:

-

-

-

KNOW HOW TO IDENTIFY A FOCUS FOR ACTION RESEARCH

Informed by your readings of 'how action research might be conceptualised' along with an increased awareness of characteristic features of the action research models identified by Kemmis, Elliott, Ebbutt and McKernan (Activity 4.1a) you have come, in part, to realise how to do action research. Within the school context, the aim of action research is to improve the quality of the teaching and learning opportunities you provide for the pupils you teach by identifying, investigating and reflecting upon an area of interest or one in need of development. In broad terms, this might be an investigation into teaching approaches to achieve a pupil-learning goal/outcome or how to improve the effectiveness of a particular teaching skill, approach or strategy. Your particular goal or focus for undertaking a study might be, for example, to examine:

- how grouping pupils according to ability, size of group and friendship affects individual performance and on-task behaviour;
- which teaching strategies are most important in promoting independent pupil learning;
- how to develop your use and range of questioning techniques to challenge the more able pupils; or
- how to develop your use of demonstration or your use of praise to enhance pupil learning.

Once you have identified the goal or focus for your investigation you need to both analyse and justify why you have chosen to investigate that particular area and begin to read relevant books and research articles. Your justification is developed from thinking about and reflecting on an aspect of your practice you have identified as an area for further development.

Literature review

A review of literature (see Activity 4.2a) is undertaken to give insight into the current body of knowledge that exists with regard to a research issue. It should include definitions of key concepts and terms, theoretical underpinnings of focal areas, and should demonstrate an understanding of findings from related research studies. For instance, in the case of the first example given above, you need to clarify, on the one hand, what you mean/understand by 'performance' and 'on-task behaviour' along with group structure and group dynamics; and, on the other, you need to search the literature to find out what research tells us about pupil performance and on-task behaviour.

This critical and analytical study of relevant literature is a vitally important aspect of action research and one that should be undertaken both to guide the formulation of a *research question* and your subsequent *plan of action*. Macintyre (2000: 16) developed a number of questions that can be asked for the purpose of comparing, contrasting and evaluating literature that might be relevant to your study:

- What was the research topic?
- What was the main theme?
- What background reading informed the study?
- What was the researcher trying to find out?
- What kind of study was it?
- How many people were involved?
- Where was the study carried out?
- What was the time scale?
- Was the participants' age/social background/willingness to be involved, important?
- How many 'action sessions' were there?
- What data gathering strategies were used?

Activity 4.2a Literature search and review

1   Select an area which needs development in relation to an aspect of your teaching or of pupil learning.
2   Conduct a literature search (library and/or web-based) on your chosen topic or area of study.
3   Produce an annotated bibliography based upon your literature search. This is characterised by accurately referencing the sources you have read/searched, along with short notes of possible use for your study which respond to relevant questions identified by Macintyre (2000) and detail content, theory, method and findings. Page number(s) are needed for any quote.
4   Write a literature review that brings together the relevant literature which compares, contrasts and discusses what has a bearing on your topic and relates to your particular goal or focus. (Be mindful not to generate a series of book reviews.) The review of literature should refer to previous research on the topic/concept in relation to established views of

    (a)   value of the topic;
    (b)   definition of the concept;
    (c)   how this relates to research on teaching.

    You need to discuss this critically and draw out that which is of value to your action research investigation.
5   Informed by your review of literature, identify a specific focus for your action research investigation and frame this within a research question.

Note: If you are unclear about conducting a literature search or writing a literature review, you can also refer to Chapters 5 and 6 in Bell (1999) for further guidance.

- What attempts were made to reduce bias?
- What evidence has been collected?
- What were the claims that were made?

and very importantly:

- Were the researchers justified in making these claims on the basis of what they had found, i.e. were the claims valid?
- What did the researchers recommend as the next step?
- What does this mean for my study?

Activity 4.2b asks you to select a topic for investigation.

KNOW HOW TO ENGAGE IN THE ACTION RESEARCH PROCESS

Plan of action

Having determined that you are going to use an action research approach for your investigation to make an improvement in a particular teaching-learning situation, decisions need to be made about what forms of data are appropriate to your investigation and how you

---

Activity 4.2b   Selecting a topic for investigation

1   Select an aspect of your teaching/pupils' learning that you would like to investigate, along with appropriate teaching strategies to promote its development.
For example, you might want to develop your ability to motivate pupils.
Appropriate teaching strategies include, e.g. providing a task-oriented
environment; treating each pupil as an individual; providing constructive
feedback to pupils; rewarding appropriate behaviour; rewarding effort as well
as success; planning tasks that are challenging but attainable with effort;
differentiating work according to individual needs, etc.

2   In relation to a real or an imaginary situation, select and justify three teaching
strategies that you want to try to develop to address the issue.

---

plan to go about collecting this data. Such decisions are made in the light of your research
question, informed by your review of relevant literature, your understanding of the cyclical
nature of the action research process and the specific research context. For example, you need
to devise a *plan of action* that considers:

- the way you are going to work with pupils to try to improve teaching and learning;
- the methods you are going to use to collect evidence about the extent of improvement
  in teaching and learning;
- the nature of the data you are going to collect;
- how you are going to analyse and interpret the evidence;
- the way in which you are going to use the result to modify your course of action in
  terms of teaching and learning.

You must monitor from the outset the way you carry out your investigation with the selected
group/s of pupils to provide a record of *ongoing research*. This is achieved by systematically
collecting data/information for the purpose of evaluation and analysis (see Activity 4.3a). The
data might, for example, be drawn from:

- field notes;
- observation schedules;
- pupil questionnaires and/or diaries;
- structured or semi-structured interviews;
- video recordings.

This information provides the basis of a lesson-by-lesson account of your action research
experience.

Data collection is crucial. The nature of the data and the collection techniques you select
should be described and justified, along with some indication of their strengths and
limitations, and a detailed account of how they are to be applied within the context of your
study. For example, how questionnaires have been constructed or a description of the pilot
run for an observation schedule (an observation can be undertaken by yourself or, for
example, your mentor or another student teacher). The data needs to be accurate (you must
record what you intend to record) so that it can be analysed and interpreted in order to
give the best possible reasons for explaining behaviours or events that occur. *Conceptual
clarity* (using precise terminology) is important as is *validity* (being able to show that
the questionnaire or observation schedule is getting the information you say that it is). The
questions you ask, how you frame them and the language you use must be appropriate.

Activity 4.3a Classroom research techniques

Conduct a literature search to identify the characteristics, possible advantages, disadvantages and uses of classroom research techniques featured in the table below (adapted from Hopkins (2002: 127)).

Technique	Characteristics	Advantage/s	Disadvantage/s	Uses
Pupil diaries	*e.g. pupils asked to complete a diary at various times*	*Gives their perceptions in their own words*	*Relies on their writing skills*	*Could be used in studies on enjoyment or understanding*
Audiotape recording				
Case study				
Documentary evidence				
Field notes				
Interviews: • structured • semi-structured • unstructured/ open • teacher/pupil • observer/pupil • pupil/pupil • group				
Observation schedules				
Sociometry, the study of social relationships				
Questionnaires: • closed questions • open questions • multiple choice questions				
Videotape recording				

The way that pupils respond to the questions is influenced by the options you provide (open, closed or multiple-choice questions) (see Activity 4.3b), how they understand and perceive the questions and, the particular climate/context when filling them in. In a similar vein, an observation schedule (see Activity 4.3c) designed to record pupils' on-task and off-task behaviour must clearly state what is meant by on-task and off-task behaviour within the given context (what specific behaviour or non-verbal communication signify the behaviour?). The validity of recordings made on this schedule are dependent upon your or your observer's ability to perceive pupil behaviour in relation to criteria that you have identified (see the Academic Learning Time (ALT-PE) observation sheets (Siedentop *et al.*, (1982)) (in Chapter 9) which look at on-task and off-task behaviour). Now complete Activity 4.3d to test your knowledge of questionnaires and interviews.

Activity 4.3b Wording questions

When designing questions, either for interview or questionnaire purposes, what you ask and how you word, phrase and sequence the questions that you ask is important. In the following exemplars, identify which questions are leading, double or restrictive in nature. Rewrite them to ensure that each has a clear focus, is not ambiguous and is not leading.

- Do you enjoy dance more than football and are you pleased with your duet choreography?
- What are the advantages and disadvantages of working in small groups for your gymnastic lessons?
- Are female PE teachers more caring than male PE teachers?
- Do you feel that school teachers fail to listen to pupils' opinions and views?

Activity 4.3c Focused observation schedules

The aim of the two prepared observation schedules below is to guide your thinking about *what* to observe, *who* to observe, *how* to observe, *when* to observe and *why*. These can be used as a springboard to inform the development of observation schedules relevant to your personal area/s of research. See also observation schedule for Academic Learning Time-Physical Education (ALT-PE) (Siedentop *et al.*, 1982) in Chapter 9.

Focused observation schedule 1: QUESTIONING

Name of Teacher/Student Teacher Observed: . . . .   Date: . . . .

Name of Observer: . . . .

Note as many questions as you can. Try to reproduce exactly what is said.

	Question	Who answers?				Comment here if question is extensive or unexpected
		Teacher	No answer	Pupils	Many pupils	
1						
2						
3						
4						
5						
6						
7						
8						
9						
10						

At end of observation fill in:

Number of *open* questions . . . .   Number of *recall* questions . . . .

Number of *pupil* questions . . . .   Number of questions *requiring thinking* . . . .

Number of *question sequences* (guided discovery) . . . .

Focused observation schedule 2: MOTIVATION

Name of Teacher/Student Teacher Observed: . . . .   Date: . . . .

Name of Observer: . . . .

Concentrate on ONE pupil throughout the lesson and complete the record for that one pupil only during each teacher episode. The teacher should not know which pupil you have chosen.

Record of praise and criticism: Name of pupil . . . .

	Instances of:		Given to:			Comments e.g. for good work or effort or improvement or behaviour or other reason
	Praise	Criticism	Individual	Group	Class	
1						
2						
3						
4						
5						
6						
7						
8						
9						
10						

Task appropriateness for this SAME pupil.

	Task	Too easy	Reasonable challenge	Too difficult	Comments
1					
2					
3					
4					
5					
6					
7					

Other comments:

Activity 4.3d Questionnaires and interviews

Read the following: Chapter 9 in Robson (1993: 227–68) and Chapters 8 and 9 in Bell (1999: 118–45). Make notes on:

- Designing and administering questionnaires;
- Planning and conducting interviews.

Account of experience

For your action research investigation two kinds of data should be collected:

1   Data to monitor what you, as the teacher, do within each lesson and to evaluate how successful you are at putting your plans into practice.
2   Data to demonstrate the effectiveness of your innovation as a whole, for example, whether pupils' on-task behaviour improves in response to your modified teaching strategies.

Data collected from these sources can be *quantitative* (numerical) or *qualitative* (generally written) and should enable you to describe and reflect on each lesson in relation to:

- key events;
- teacher, pupil and/or observer behaviour;
- problems encountered;
- necessary adjustments to the action plan and/or refinements to data collection techniques.

In light of your response to the above issues, you should plan what to do next and the data you need to collect. You must record this process with clarity and consistency throughout your investigation, indicating the basis upon which changes were made to the strategy and used to modify and develop your teaching and pupil learning from lesson to lesson through *formative evaluation*. Your results and discussions provide opportunities for reflection and the cross-referencing of findings. What is important in this record of ongoing research is the clear explanation of a development based upon sound evidence and the quality of the conclusions you have drawn.

Collation and analysis of data

Once you have completed your action research investigation, you need to present, interpret and analyse your findings. You should collate your raw data and organise your research evidence into categories that are appropriate. For example, in the case of a study which has used focused observation schedule 2 on Motivation (Activity 4.3b), you should begin to categorise findings in relation to: instances of individual praise; instances of group praise; instances of class praise, and so on. Findings can be presented in the form of summaries of your data rather than the raw data itself, along with tables, graphs, transcripts of significant conversations and/or records of illuminating incidents. Having established appropriate categories, you can examine the findings and look for evidence of similarities and differences, groupings, patterns, trends and events/incidents that are of particular significance to your research question and focus. You should be able to survey all the data you have collected over the research weeks to interpret, analyse and critically reflect on your overall findings.

The validity and usefulness of your findings for teaching should be judged realistically and be considered in the light of prior reading and relevant research. You need to recognise that your findings have arisen from a specific context, one that involves you as the researcher focusing on a particular aspect of teaching and/or pupil learning, with a particular group of pupils in a particular environment. Care needs to be exercised to avoid making claims or generalisations based upon limited data that has emerged from a small-scale investigation.

Triangulation is often used in action research as one of several techniques designed to measure the 'trustworthiness' or *validity* of a category or hypothesis. It is characterised by collecting data about a particular teaching-learning situation from three quite different perspectives: usually those of the pupils, an observer and the teacher/researcher. In this way different sources of data can be cross-referenced to validate whether something has occurred.

For example, if you claim that your study has promoted inclusion, you should also ask: 'Does the pupil's account fit with observer and teacher data?', 'Does the pupil feel included?', 'On what observations and data are you claiming that she is included and that your strategy has worked?'

In drawing conclusions you might suggest changes that, if you were to undertake your study again, you could make to improve some aspect of the research. Also, you might consider whether your findings have relevance to other teaching and learning situations. Perceived limitations of your study should be identified and you might recommend possible future research and developments.

SUMMARY

By working through this chapter you will understand how action research might be conceptualised; how to identify a focus for action research; and how to engage in the action research process. This should enable you to conduct your own action research study to support your development into a reflective practitioner and therefore a more effective teacher.

ACKNOWLEDGEMENT

Some ideas for the approach used in this chapter arose from work by Margaret Whitehead.

Part 2   Knowing your content

Chapter 5   Long-term planning of the physical education curriculum

PETER BRECKON AND CATHY GOWER

INTRODUCTION

All the planned experiences that contribute to pupils' learning and development within the context and ethos of the school are generally referred to as the school curriculum. To plan a physical education curriculum effectively you need to understand the mechanics of planning at three different levels: planning in the long-term (schemes of work); planning in the medium-term (units of work); and planning in the short-term (lesson plans). However, definitions of what constitutes planning, in particular long- and medium-term planning, differ, resulting in an interchangeable use of terminology and subsequent confusion over how the physical education experience is or should be planned. Using the web page http:/www.standards. dfes.gov.uk/schemes3/planning make sure you are clear about the differences between long-, medium- and short-term planning; between planning schemes and units of work in physical education.

Although it is unlikely that at this stage of your teaching career you will be involved in long-term planning, in this chapter we consider the influences that shape a school's overall physical education curriculum. In Chapter 6 we consider medium- and short-term planning.

By the end of this chapter you should be able to:

- understand the factors that influence planning in physical education and engage in a critical review of existing planning models;
- understand the constraints on a physical education curriculum and planning issues that result;
- analyse a physical education curriculum and determine the extent to which it presents pupils with a broad and balanced experience and takes account of continuity and progression;
- undertake the long-term planning of a physical education curriculum, taking account of statutory requirements.

Each school has a physical education policy which outlines the aims (the long-term intentions of the subject) and describes the objectives (the stepping stones or ways in which they work towards achieving those aims) of the subject. In writing the policy, staff have considered many factors which have an influence on the physical education curriculum experienced by pupils in the school, including:

- the school's ethos, values and aims;
- the ethos, values and aims of the physical education department;
- the requirements of the National Curriculum for Physical Education (NCPE);

- the wider demands of the National Curriculum;
- the need to provide a broad and balanced curriculum that has both continuity and progression;
- the available facilities.

However, before considering the influence of this variety of factors, it is important that you engage in a critical review of existing perspectives on planning in physical education (see Activity 5.1).

While undertaking Activity 5.1 you probably recognise some of the influences that affected the planning of the curriculum that you experienced as a pupil. As a result of this, it is likely that you bring with you certain philosophies and beliefs about your subject area which influence your views of teaching and learning in physical education (see Chapter 3).

THE SCHOOL'S ETHOS, VALUES AND AIMS

Physical education, like all subjects, has to justify its place in what is seen by many to be an over-crowded curriculum. The value a school places on different subject areas is reflected in the priority – and in particular the time, given to them (see Activity 5.2).

THE ETHOS, VALUES AND AIMS OF THE PHYSICAL EDUCATION DEPARTMENT

Another factor often considered significant is the traditions of the school and the expertise and interests of the members of staff. It is quite common for a school to recruit staff with particular expertise in an activity area in which the school is strong or wishes to develop a strength. Such factors have an influence on both the formal curriculum and the range of extra-curricular activities offered (see Activity 5.3). The advantage of this is that the school often develops a reputation in this activity and the enthusiasm of the members of staff has a positive effect on pupils' attitudes. The disadvantage is that there can be an imbalance and pupils miss out on experiencing a variety of contexts.

THE REQUIREMENTS OF THE NCPE

Schools are guided to various degrees in what they are expected to teach. Within this context, NCPE 2000 (DfEE/QCA, 1999) clearly defines what should underpin planning into what pupils should learn and do in physical education. It does this through the organising principle of a learning-based curriculum in which the activity (the product) is given less emphasis than the four strands related to pupil learning (the process):

- acquiring and developing skills;
- selecting and applying skills, tactics and compositional ideas;
- evaluating and improving performance;
- knowledge and understanding of fitness and health.

Although the NCPE also specifies within the Programmes of Study the areas of activity that need to be taught at each Key Stage, these represent the context of pupil learning. It is through these areas of activity that the four strands of pupil learning in physical education must be delivered.

The four strands make up the Attainment Target for physical education. This is divided into levels, each level providing a description of the achievements of pupils working at that level in relation to each of the strands.

It can therefore be seen that curriculum planning needs to take account of both the four strands of attainment and the areas of activity in order to fulfil the statutory requirements (see Activity 5.4).

Activity 5.1 Perspectives on curriculum planning in physical education

Note the perspective in each of the readings below. Compare and contrast these perspectives.

Reference	Perspectives on planning in physical education
Department of Education and Science/Welsh Office (DES/WO, 1991)	
Department for Education and Employment/Qualifications and Curriculum Authority (DfEE/QCA, 1999)	
Murdoch (1997, 2004)	
Penney (2001)	
Penney and Chandler (2000)	
Penney and Evans (2000)	
Talbot (1993)	
Department of National Heritage (1995)	

Activity 5.2 How people within the school view physical education

Record the evidence from the various sources identified in the table below that give you insights into the value placed on physical education in the school and how it might influence the way in which the physical education curriculum is planned.

Form of evidence	Summary of findings
Documents, e.g. school's prospectus, notice boards, newsletter, local paper	
Attitude of the headteacher towards physical education	
Attitude of the senior management team towards physical education	
Attitudes of the governors towards physical education	
Community links	
Extent of staff and pupil involvement in extra-curricular activities	
Success of school in interschool competitions	

Activity 5.3 Factors which influence the scheme of work in a physical education department

Question	Response
How do available facilities and equipment influence the design of the scheme of work?	
How is the NCPE interpreted within the department's scheme of work?	
Do personal areas of expertise within the department determine what is included within the scheme?	
How does the scheme of work cater for the needs of different groups of pupils and individuals within those groups?	
How does the department's scheme of work respond to the Key Stage 3 Strategy and learning across the curriculum?	
What whole-school factors influence the scheme of work?	
What government documents have been utilised to support the planning process and why and how?	
What other resources and sources of support are utilised when devising the department's scheme of work?	

Activity 5.4   How the four strands are 'mapped' into documents that inform the work of the department

Note the extent to which the four strands are represented within physical education documents. Some are listed below, but also include other documents, as appropriate.

Documents	Representation of the four strands
Aims of the department	
Units of work	
Learning outcomes of lessons	
Assessment policy	
Reports to parents	

THE WIDER DEMANDS OF THE NATIONAL CURRICULUM

Changing demands and new initiatives are influencing what we teach and how we teach it. Many of these place additional demands on the teacher, particularly the need to contribute to pupils' wider education through planned contributions to other aspects of learning (see Chapters 6 and 7).

A BROAD AND BALANCED CURRICULUM THAT HAS BOTH CONTINUITY AND PROGRESSION

When the National Curriculum for England was introduced in 1988, one of its explicit aims was to ensure that pupils experience 'a broad and balanced curriculum whilst demonstrating continuity and progression' (DES, 1987: 4). The application of these concepts in terms of the long-term planning in physical education is explored below.

Curriculum breadth and balance

If a school is meeting the requirements of the NCPE in terms of the areas of activity they are offering pupils, then they should be providing a broad curriculum. The current requirements are that during Key Stage 3, pupils should be taught the knowledge, skills and understanding as exemplified within the four strands of attainment at an appropriate level through four areas of activity, including games, and three others, at least one of which must be dance or gymnastic activities. During Key Stage 4, pupils should be taught the knowledge, skills and understanding through two of the six activity areas.

Having decided the areas of activity through which the strands of the physical education curriculum will be delivered, it is necessary to decide how much time is to be devoted to each. However, as well as the amount of time devoted to each area of activity, balance refers to many other aspects of the curriculum, including, perhaps most importantly, the balance of planning for pupil attainment across all four strands. Other areas of balance which may be considered are the balance of competitive (e.g. games) and non-competitive/co-operative activities (e.g. dance, OAA) or the balance of individual and team activities. Balance could also be looked at in terms of the demands made upon the body, i.e. the extent to which curriculum planning ensures that over the long-term there is a balanced use of the body.

Physical education departments, however, rarely have the luxury of providing totally the curriculum they would like to achieve balance. Facilities are one of the constraints. For example the amount of indoor and outdoor space and availability of facilities such as a swimming pool affect the range of activities available. Some facilities become unavailable at various times of the year. For example large indoor spaces are often used for examinations and drama productions. Similarly, outdoor spaces may become unusable in the winter time. The Office for Standards in Education (OfSTED, 2002: 3) noted that 'one in five schools have inadequate access to specialist accommodation; a lack of indoor work areas, and outdoor play areas with poor drainage and poor standards of maintenance inhibit the programme that schools can offer'. It is important that for long-term planning purposes these constraints are taken account of. For example, by teaching indoor activities when the weather is likely to be inappropriate for teaching outside activities, such as the first half of the spring term (see Activity 5.5).

OfSTED (2002: 3) noted that, 'Although in over half of schools there is a well-planned curriculum, the time allocation still favours games more than other aspects; to some extent this reflects limitations in accommodation, but also teacher preference.' Activity 5.6 asks you to identify the balance of work in the physical education curriculum.

Continuity and progression

In considering long-term planning it is also necessary to consider curriculum continuity and progression. Using a dictionary definition of continuity as being a 'consistent line of development without any sharp breaks', Murdoch (2004: 287) considers that learning should be 'one logical, focused, seamless, smooth state of growth or advancement'. The important point is that planning should take account of what has gone before so that new knowledge, skills and understanding build on previous learning in a logical sequence.

Progression, on the other hand, concerns the sequencing of the content. It is based on the structures of the subject, with pupils progressing from initial to more mature forms of knowledge, skills and understanding. The concept is, according to Murdoch (ibid.: 288), 'that

Note all the activities that are taught in the curriculum at Key Stages 3 and 4.

Year	Autumn Term		Spring Term		Summer Term	
	Activity	No. of weeks/time	Activity	No. of weeks/time	Activity	No. of weeks/time
7						
8						
9						
10						
11						

Total time spent on each area of activity:

Area of activity	Hours: Key Stage 3	Hours: Key Stage 4
Athletics		
Dance		
Games		
Gymnastics		
Outdoor and Adventurous Activities		
Swimming		

Activity 5.6   Balance in the physical education curriculum

Using the data you gathered for Activity 5.5, as well as the school's schemes of work for physical education, complete the following table in relation to the various dimensions of balance identified above.

Question	Answer
Is there a balance in focus within the four strands over the long-term?	
Do any of the activities through which the strands are delivered receive a larger proportion of time than others?	
What is the balance of competitive and co-operative activities?	
Is there a balance of individual and team activities?	
Does the curriculum ensure there is a balanced use of the body?	

Using your findings, ask the following questions:

Question	Answer
What are the reasons for the differences in curriculum balance?	
What is the rationale for choosing the activities offered?	
What are the practical constraints on offering certain areas of activity? e.g. staff expertise or lack of facilities	

Activity 5.7 Critical analysis of the extent to which continuity and progression exist within the physical education curriculum

Using the school's schemes of work for a Key Stage, look critically at the continuity and progression within one area of activity. Ask the following questions:

- Is the activity continuous over all years within the Key Stage?
- Does planning of the area of activity over the Key Stage show progression across all four strands?
- Do you feel the amount of time devoted to the activity per unit of work allows progression?
- What changes would you make to ensure better continuity and progression within this area of activity?

There is a proforma on the website (http://www.routledge.com/textbooks/0415361117) that you may want to use to help you undertake this activity.

learning should take place over an extended period in steady stages that empower the learner to achieve more complex, better things'. Planning for progression is therefore a major aspect of any curriculum development. Effective planning involves carefully and deliberately sequencing the curriculum content and experiences that teachers intend learners to have. These plans should build on previous learning and achievements to promote future learning.

Thus, continuity and progression as exemplified within the NCPE strands of the attainment target and programmes of study should be evident at the long-term planning stage (see Activity 5.7).

SUMMARY

This chapter has looked at long-term planning in physical education. It has considered many of the factors that govern planning decisions. You have been asked to analyse, challenge and seek justifications for decisions made about the physical education curriculum. In undertaking this process you will have come to the realisation that there are many constraints on the curriculum and that a number of factors prevent us from delivering our ideal curriculum. In the next chapter we consider how our long-term plans can be transferred into medium-term units of work and short-term individual lesson plans.

FURTHER READING

Several further readings are identified in Activity 5.1 . See also:

Murdoch, E. (2004) NCPE 2000 – Where are we so far? In S. Capel (ed.) *Learning to Teach Physical Education in the Secondary School: A Companion to School Experience*, London: RoutledgeFalmer, pp. 280–300. This chapter provides a very useful guide to help you understand the essential aspects of progression from one level to another.

Chapter 6 Medium- and short-term planning in physical education

PETER BRECKON AND CATHY GOWER

INTRODUCTION

In Chapter 5 we considered influences that shape the overall physical education curriculum of a school and hence pupils' total learning experiences. We also considered the mechanics of long-term planning in the National Curriculum for Physical Education (NCPE). In this chapter we turn our attention to the next two levels of planning – medium and short-term – or unit of work and lesson planning. As a student teacher you have little influence on the long-term planning of the physical education curriculum. However, you are required to be able to plan sequences of lessons and individual lessons in the form of units of work and lesson plans.

By the end of this chapter you should be able to:

- articulate the relationship between medium- and short-term planning in physical education;
- identify a range of factors which need to be taken into account when planning units of work and lesson plans;
- map NCPE requirements into your medium- and short-term planning;
- write specific and assessable intended learning outcomes (ILOs) and learning activities for both units of work and lesson plans which cross-refer to the four NCPE strands;
- cater for a range of preferred learning styles in planned learning activities;
- draw on the expertise of experienced teachers to plan effective physical education lessons.

MEDIUM-TERM PLANNING

Units of work are medium-term planning documents that outline expected learning for particular groups of pupils within a year group and possibly for a particular area of activity over a specified period of time. Before you begin to plan your unit of work, you need to find out where the sequence of lessons fits into the overall scheme of work for the Key Stage. The way in which the NCPE document (DFEE/QCA, 1999) is constructed reflects a linear approach to curriculum planning. The long-term overview of learning (the scheme of work) is used to inform the writing of medium-term plans (units of work). These outline expectations for learning for an identified group of pupils over a specified period of time. Units of work are then used to help shape expectations for learning in the short-term (lesson plans).

There are many different models for planning schemes and units of work and lesson plans within physical education. A curriculum planning model that has been adopted by many schools and physical education departments has been devised by the Department for Education and Skills (DfES) and QCA. This model can be viewed at the following website:

http://www.standards.dfes.gov.uk/schemes2/Secondary_PE. The DfES and QCA schemes and units of work for physical education are intended as guidance documents to be adapted according to the specific needs of each individual school. It is important that you see them as a source of support, but still engage in critical thinking about how to plan to meet the specific needs of the pupils you are working with in your particular context.

Prior to the introduction of these exemplar materials, it was common for departments to adopt a unit planning model which described lesson by lesson what pupils would learn, or more realistically in terms of the way in which they were written, what a pupil would actually do (e.g. for basketball it might be: passing week one; dribbling week two; set shot week three, etc.). Such an approach to unit planning has been criticised for outlining learning in an activity-specific way, thus failing to promote what Penney and Chandler (2000) refer to as 'connectivity' in learning. It can also fail to help pupils meet NCPE requirements across the four strands of *acquiring and developing skills* (A&D), *selecting and applying skills, tactics and compositional ideas* (S&A), *evaluating and improving performance* (E&I) and *knowledge and understanding about health and fitness* (F&H). Without explicit planning for the four strands, the focus for learning tends to be mainly on the strand of A&D at the expense of the other strands. In fact, the Office for Standards in Education (OfSTED, 2003) identified that curriculum planning and design in physical education do not equitably address all four NCPE strands. It also often fails to take account of planning for progression and continuity in pupil learning. Unit planning should take account of prior attainment in order to ensure, as much as is possible, the correct pitch for pupil learning in relation to the four NCPE strands. This then provides a framework for planning. However, units which specify what pupils will do lesson by lesson are not always flexible enough to adjust to learning that has/has not taken place in the previous lesson.

Therefore, a unit of work should outline the knowledge, skills and understanding that the teacher intends the pupils to acquire over a set period of time appropriately pitched and taking account of prior attainment, but be flexible enough to adjust expectations as you go along in order to take account of the developing needs of the group (see Activity 6.1).

WRITING INTENDED LEARNING OUTCOMES FOR A UNIT

Without doubt, the most important aspect of writing a unit of work is formulating your objectives or intentions for pupils' learning. In this chapter these objectives or intentions are referred to as ILOs. However, other terminology may be used on your ITE programme. Likewise, in this chapter the ILOs are written for the whole class, and achievement of pupils against the ILOs forms part of the formative and summative assessment of pupils. However, on other courses, it is the ILOs themselves that are differentiated to cater for the range of pupils in the class. The examples in Chapter 12 divide ILOs into three bands: those that can be achieved by most of the pupils in the class, with different ILOs for pupils who cannot achieve those and for those pupils who need to be extended further. On the other courses you may be asked to write ILOs for different aspects of pupils' learning, e.g. in terms of the knowledge pupils will acquire, the skills they will be able to perform, and what development in their understanding will result from the unit. ILOs are specific and assessable statements about what your pupils will achieve by the end of the unit (see also Chapters 7 and 11). OfSTED (2003: 5) highlighted 'Trainees' inability to consistently define objectives for learning with precision continued to undermine their ability to judge and record progress'. Thus, the ability to write specific and assessable ILOs is a crucial area for development in your ITE. Defining ILOs for learning is an essential part of planning in both the medium and short-term.

A useful model for planning is one that ensures that ILOs include a *verb*, *context* and *quality* to describe what pupils will know, do and understand, the context in which it will be demonstrated, and the quality you will be looking for to assess achievement of the ILO. The *verb* used in any ILO should directly relate to the targeted strand (e.g. travel – A&D; devise – S&A; describe – E&I; adopt – F&H). The ability to relate verbs to specific strands should

Make notes on how the factors listed below that you need to take into account when planning a unit of work have been used to inform planning within a unit of work taken from the school's scheme of work and a corresponding one taken from the QCA scheme. Two examples have been provided.

Example – Title of unit – Year 7 Athletics

Factors which need to be taken into account when planning a unit of work	How does the department take these factors into account in the selected unit?	How are these factors represented in the QCA units?
What recognition/information is provided of prior learning?	*The department holds centrally records of the level pupils have achieved in each area of activity*	*The unit contains a section on 'prior learning'*
Are the ILOs for pupil learning mapped against all four NCPE strands?	*All strands are represented but most weight is given to the A&D strand and tends to be event-specific in the athletics unit*	*The planned outcomes take account of all four strands*

Title of unit . . . .

Factors which need to be taken into account when planning a unit of work	How does the department take these factors into account in the selected unit?	How are these factors represented in the QCA units?
What recognition/information is provided of prior learning?		
Are the ILOs for pupil learning mapped against all four NCPE strands?		
Do the ILOs provide clear criteria to assess pupil learning, identifying aspects of quality expected in pupils' responses?		
How much time is available to teach the unit?		

What resources are required/available to teach the unit?		
How is the work to be assessed?		
What is to be taught later?		
To what extent are broader aspects of pupil learning represented in the unit planning (e.g. language for learning, key skills)?		
What detail is given concerning the teaching strategies to be used and do these take account of a range of different learning styles?		
Are examples provided of learning activities that could be used?		
What other information is provided that is not included above?		

To help you to develop your vocabulary for planning across all four NCPE strands, sort into the table below the following verbs according to whether you feel they relate to A&D, S&A, E&I or F&H:

acquire	develop	select
know	understand	link
criticise	prioritise	copy
recognise	adapt	modify
plan	respond	manipulate
compose	react	decide
observe	copy	prepare
evaluate	relate	improve
perform	organise	analyse
identify	combine	reflect
create	name	appreciate
express	explain	coordinate
change	use	control
communicate	choose	interpret
apply	consolidate	anticipate
extend	define	judge
describe	name	design
refine	recall	devise
extend	state	suggest
solve	relate	show
express	justify	comment
compare	distinguish	assess
discuss	predict	resolve
categorise	summarise	appraise
contrast	discriminate	outline
list	label	reproduce
present	extract	recount
examine	question	diagnose

A&D	S&A	E&I	F&H

help to identify outcomes for all strands. This overcomes the concern of OfSTED (2002: 5) that: 'Curricular planning needs to satisfy the four aspects of knowledge, skills and understanding in the National Curriculum across different areas of activity' (see Activities 6.2, 6.3 and 6.4).

Were there any occasions where it was difficult to allocate a verb to a particular strand? Why do you think this was the case? Were there occasions where you placed a verb in more than one column? Why do you think this occurred?

Activity 6.3 Key words in ILOs

Use three different colour highlighter pens to identify the distinct elements of the *verb*, *context*, *quality* framework in each unit of work ILO below, i.e. pink = verb, yellow = context, blue = quality.

Year 8: Net games unit of work – 12 hours duration

By the end of this unit of work pupils will be able to:

- Demonstrate disguise in a badminton shot using pushing, tapping and whipping type actions which vary the weight, distance, angle and trajectory of the shuttle as it travels in practice and adapted game situation (A&D).
- Play a range of different shots on both sides of the body in practice and adapted game situations showing a return to base position, side on body position, efficient use of footwork and balance within preparation, execution and follow-through phases (A&D).
- Set up an attack in adapted game situations by moving your opponent out of position, playing on their weaknesses, forcing them to the extremes of the court, limiting their recovery time and sending them the wrong way (S&A).
- Win a point in adapted game situations by choosing an appropriate opportunity by exploiting your opponent's weaknesses, placing the shuttle out of reach, reducing time available to get to the shuttle and forcing them to the limits of their technical ability (S&A).
- Defend space on your own court and defend against an attack in adapted game situations by covering weak areas on the court, recovering to base position and using shot selection to create time and regain the initiative (S&A).
- Use an appropriate language from a given set of criteria to describe strengths in both technical and strategic play for a given model of performance (E&I).
- Select the best place to observe the performance of a range of shots by a partner in practice and adapted game situations based on the type of shot and the body position required to execute it (E&I).
- Analyse own or a partner's response in practices and adapted game situations using a set criteria focusing upon either setting up an attack, defending against an attack or winning the point defending space, and provide constructive, objective and sensitive feedback using appropriate terminology (E&I).
- Explain what they need to do to improve their own fitness level to be a more effective net games player (F&H).
- Identify areas of fitness most needed in net games and explain how involvement in these games contributes to their fitness, health and well-being (F&H).
- Carry out warm-up and cool-down routines safely (F&H).
- Select and incorporate pulse raising, stretching and mobilisation exercises which are suitable for net games (F&H).

Activity 6.4 Writing ILOs for a selected unit of work using the *verb*, *context*, *quality* framework

Write the ILOs for a unit of work you are going to teach utilising the *verb*, *context*, *quality* framework. Ensure these ILOs include a balance of the four NCPE strands.

PLANNING LEARNING ACTIVITIES FOR UNITS OF WORK

Once you have planned your ILOs, it is important to plan a range of learning activities that promote learning across the four NCPE strands and therefore promote the multidimensional nature of learning in physical education. We also have to ensure that when planning learning activities we draw on learning theory which identifies preferences in terms of the way in which we learn. For example, in recent years we have seen the emergence in education of Accelerated Learning (Rose, 1985) which is based on theories such as Gardner's (1993) *Theory of Multiple Intelligences* and Kolb's (1984) *Theory of Experiential Learning*. Accelerated learning has seen a simplification of such theories to the identification of three main preferred learning styles: visual, auditory and kinaesthetic (VAK). Part of your professional development involves an exploration of the relationship between theory and practice and thus the understanding of how such theory can apply to the planning, delivery and assessment of learning experiences in physical education (see Activity 6.5).

In Activity 6.6 a unit of work for year group 8 playing badminton is developed fully. Study the lesson plan and think about opportunities to promote pupils' learning in broader curriculum areas that typically arise within your teaching. How will you utilise them in future?

So far, we have explored factors which need to be taken into account when planning a unit of work, how to construct clear and assessable ILOs cross-referenced to the NCPE strands and how to research related learning activities which cater for different types of learner (see Activity 6.7).

Activity 6.5 Mapping learning activities against the NCPE strands and different preferred learning styles

To establish the pitch of a unit of work you are going to teach, take account of pupils' prior learning and their expectations in relation to the NCPE level descriptions (DfEE/QCA, 1999). Using a range of resources such as textbooks, websites, DVDs, videos, etc., plan a variety of learning activities which can be mapped against the NCPE strands and which cater for different learning styles. Complete the background information and then write your learning activities in the table provided:

Activity: . . . .   Year group:

Prior learning: . . . .
. . . .
. . . .

The majority of pupils are working at national curriculum level: . . . .

The related QCA unit of work would be: . . . .

	Visual	Auditory	Kinaesthetic
Acquiring and developing			
Selecting and applying			
Evaluating and improving			
Knowledge and understanding of fitness and health			

Activity 6.6 Unit of work for Year 8

UNIT OF WORK

AREA OF ACTIVITY Games (badminton)	**KEY STAGE** 3
YEAR GROUP Eight	**DURATION** 12 hours
RESOURCES Four badminton courts 30 shuttles, 30 racquets, 30 short tennis racquets, 30 tennis balls, 30 sponge balls and TV and video Worksheets	**LANGUAGE FOR LEARNING** Side-on body position, base position, balance, footwork patterns, preparation, execution, follow-through, pushing, tapping, whipping, set-up and attack, defend space or against attack, win the point, observation criteria, sensitivity, objective, manoeuvre opponent out of position, identify strengths and weaknesses, force to extremes of court, recovery time, regain initiative
PRIOR LEARNING This is the group's first experience of net games and badminton. They are an attaining group of Year 8s with expectations for all strands pitched at level 4/5. Worksheets with visual and verbal prompts will be needed to support a high proportion of EAL pupils. Key words to be identified and highlighted every lesson. Pupil A is gifted and talented in relation to net games (county tennis player). However, needs to work on E&I still in all areas of activity	**KEY SKILLS** Communication, problem solving, working with others, improving own learning and performance

INTENDED LEARNING OUTCOMES	LEARNING ACTIVITIES	TEACHING METHODS
ACQUIRING AND DEVELOPING Pupils will be able to: • Demonstrate disguise in a badminton shot using pushing, tapping and whipping actions which vary the weight, distance, angle and trajectory of the shuttle as it travels in practice and adapted game situations • Play a range of different shots on both sides of the body in practice and adapted game situations showing a return-to-base position, side-on body position, efficient use of footwork and balance within preparation, execution and follow-through phases	Observe model techniques or own/others' technique on video to explore commonalities/differences in the movement of the body across a range of shots Introductory activities which use balls and shuttles exploring best body position to send an object Individual racquet and shuttle familiarisation activities exploring different grips, pushing, tapping and whipping actions and use of forehand and backhand Pupils create individual sequences of shots and repeat them, considering through Q&A how they are changing what they do with their body, the racquet and the shuttle to vary them, i.e. variations in degree of preparation and follow through Pupils teach each other sequences, their individual sequences of shots and use appropriate terminology to provide input and feedback Use of worker, feeder, retriever, observer formats to explore different shot actions, i.e. pushing, tapping, whipping actions. Format should alter intensity of feeding process, level of predictability, speed of feeding, target for worker, etc. Use of worksheets to provide observation criteria	Teacher-led activities using demonstration, explanation and verbal feedback Video analysis Guided-discovery Pupils reciprocally teaching using worksheets Differentiation by task and outcome

Activity 6.6 *continued*

INTENDED LEARNING OUTCOMES	LEARNING ACTIVITIES	TEACHING METHODS
SELECTING AND APPLYING Pupils will be able to: • Set up an attack in adapted game situations by moving their opponent out of position, playing on their weaknesses, forcing them to the extremes of the court, limiting their recovery time and sending them the wrong way • Win a point in adapted game situations by choosing an appropriate opportunity by exploiting their opponent's weaknesses, placing the shuttle out of reach, reducing time available to get to the shuttle and forcing them to the limits of their technical ability • Defend space on their own court and defend against an attack in adapted game situations by covering weak areas on the court, recovering to base position and using shot selection to create time and regain the initiative	Use of video to analyse models of performance, i.e. Olympic medal-winning pair Use of worksheets which focus on analysing different aspects of play, i.e. setting up an attack Pupils invent their own net game using different types of equipment but with common central aim. Explore through this similarities and differences between principles of all net games Use different games using various types of equipment but with central net games aim Set up adapted game situations which vary the space in which pupils work, i.e. long thin court or short fat court according to aim of game Set up adapted game situations which vary the scoring system to emphasise certain aspects of play, i.e. rewarding effective defensive play Set up adapted game situations which are initially co-operative and then progress to becoming competitive Set up game situations which have particular focused goals, i.e. score by landing shuttle between tram lines at back of court Set up game situations which have different numbers of players to emphasise different aspects of play, i.e. 4 vs 4, two deep players responsible for deep-court play and two front-court players responsible for front court play	Teacher-led activities Guided discovery/ Games for understanding Video analysis Pupil observation, analysis and feedback Differentiation by task and outcome
EVALUATING AND IMPROVING Pupils will be able to: • Use an appropriate language from a given set of criteria to describe strengths in both technical and strategic play for a given model of performance • Select the best place to observe the performance of a range of shots by a partner in practice and adapted game situations based on the type of shot and the body position required to execute it • Analyse own or a partner's response in practice and adapted game situations using a set criterion focusing upon either setting up an attack, defending against an attack, or winning the point, defending space, and provide constructive, objective and sensitive feedback using appropriate terminology	Use of video analysis with individual, partner, small-group and whole-class-related activities and supporting worksheets with observational prompts Use of video analysis of pupil performance using key words on board or on worksheets Use of split-screen video analysis to support comparison of techniques, i.e. model–pupil, pupil–pupil Use of quad format, as in A&D, to rotate in observing pupils, to analyse either technical or strategic responses in practice and game situations	Pupil observation, analysis and feedback opportunities Guided discovery/ games for understanding Demonstrations Reciprocal teaching Video analysis

Activity 6.6 *continued*

INTENDED LEARNING OUTCOMES	LEARNING ACTIVITIES	TEACHING METHODS
KNOWLEDGE AND UNDERSTANDING ABOUT FITNESS AND HEALTH Pupils will be able to: • Explain what they need to do to improve their own fitness level to be a more effective net games player • Identify areas of fitness most needed in net games and explain how involvement in these games contributes to their fitness, health and well-being • Carry out warm-up and cool-down routines safely • Select and incorporate pulse-raising, stretching and mobilisation exercises which are suitable for net games	Pulse-raising activities such as teacher-led footwork patterns for net games with pupils mirroring actions Teacher-led stretches and mobilisations using a racquet Pupils in groups on different courts in base position, lines of court called out by teacher, pupils use footwork patterns to run and touch line with foot and then recover to base position Pair warm-ups/cool-downs with describer/demonstrator and doer/evaluator Small group warm-ups/cool-downs with each pupil taking it in turns to describe/demonstrate pulse-raiser, stretches and mobilisations and rest do/evaluate Group game where member runs to front and turns over card with description of joint/muscle required for net games and why. Member returns to group, outlines muscle and requirement and then the group have to devise and perform appropriate warm-up activity for this muscle/joint Group pulse-raising game with aim to place as many shuttles as possible in opponent's court (throwing only) in time limit with set number of shuttles allocated to each team	Teacher- led warm-ups/cool-downs Pupil led warm-ups/cool-downs Demonstration/ explanation Question and answer

Activity 6.7 Writing a unit of work

Using the example of a unit of work on net games based on the ILOs you encountered earlier in this chapter, select a group and identified area of activity you are required to teach and write a unit of work using this format.

UNIT OF WORK		
AREA OF ACTIVITY:	KEY STAGE:	
YEAR GROUP:	DURATION:	
RESOURCES:	LANGUAGE FOR LEARNING:	
PRIOR LEARNING:	KEY SKILLS:	
INTENDED LEARNING OUTCOMES	LEARNING ACTIVITIES	TEACHING AND LEARNING STRATEGIES
ACQUIRING AND DEVELOPING		
SELECTING AND APPLYING		
EVALUATING AND IMPROVING		
KNOWLEDGE AND UNDERSTANDING OF HEALTH AND FITNESS		

SHORT-TERM PLANNING

The unit plan provides a framework for a series of lessons. The unit ILOs are the initial focus for your short-term lesson planning, since these are the criteria against which you assess pupils during and/or at the end of the unit. Therefore, it is important that that you use your unit ILOs to directly inform your intentions for pupil learning in lessons – see the example of the relationship between unit and lesson ILOs in a gymnastic unit of work.

Year 7 Gymnastics Unit of Work	
Unit ILO	Related lesson ILO
By the end of this unit pupils will be able to:	By the end of this lesson pupils will be able to:
Acquire and develop	
Perform a range of body actions (e.g. jumps, rolls and weight on hands movements) and balances on the floor and apparatus showing good body tension, extension and clarity of body shape	Perform a variety or rolls on the floor from different starting and finishing positions, demonstrating good body tension and clarity of body shape
Select and apply	
Select and apply, on the floor and apparatus, a range of actions and balances to produce individual sequences in which the end of one movement becomes the beginning of the next. These should demonstrate contrasts in body shape, level, speed and pathway	Devise and perform individually a sequence consisting of three rolls, two balances and a jump demonstrating variations in body shape and changes in speed so that the end of one movement becomes the beginning of the next
Evaluate and improve	
Identify aspects relating to the strengths and weaknesses of a partner's sequence using criteria provided by the teacher and give constructive feedback, demonstrating the ability to use appropriate terminology	Provide verbal feedback to a partner on the quality of his/her sequence, focusing on the clarity of body shape. In providing this feedback the pupils should speak clearly and demonstrate the use of appropriate terminology. (e.g. *clear shape, tucked roll, stretched jump*)
Knowledge and understanding of health and fitness	
Demonstrate safe practice when lifting, supporting and manoeuvring people and equipment in skill practices and when devising sequences of movement	Support a partner during a variety of counterbalances demonstrating a solid base and appropriate posture to prevent injury

When analysing the relationship between these unit and lesson ILOs, you will note that the unit ILOs are broader in terms of the range of possible contexts and also the aspects of quality expected to be seen in the response. The lesson ILOs are far more specific in terms of both the learning context and identified aspects of quality (see Activity 6.8.)

Activity 6.8 Relating unit ILOs to lesson ILOs

In the following table in relation to an area of activity you will be teaching, write a lesson ILO for each of the four strands that relates to a unit ILO.

Area of activity . . . . Level at which the unit is pitched . . . .

Unit ILO	Related lesson ILO
By the end of this unit pupils will be able to:	By the end of this lesson pupils will be able to:
Acquire and develop	
Select and apply	
Evaluate and improve	
Knowledge and understanding of health and fitness	

Having stated clearly what you want pupils to learn in your lesson, you are now in a position to identify the sequence of learning experiences you will provide to give all pupils the opportunity to succeed. It is generally accepted that experienced teachers do not plan lessons in the same detail as student teachers, at least not explicitly. Indeed, when looking at differences in planning between beginning teachers and experienced teachers Griffey and Housner (1999) noted that the latter planned in much less depth and were more able to deviate from their planned activities based on the process of formative assessment (see assessment for learning in Chapter 12) during the lesson. Beginning teachers, on the other hand, with less experience to call upon, needed to think through carefully every aspect of the lesson and lacked the experience to adapt plans during the lesson (see Activity 6.9).

Activity 6.9 Observing and analysing lessons delivered by experienced teachers

This activity is designed to help you to 'unpick' much of the implicit planning that experienced teachers develop. Ask an experienced teacher if you can observe a lesson. Before the lesson, complete the details below and discuss the ILOs with the teacher. While you are observing, complete the columns for each learning activity that take place. An explanation of what to include in each column is written below.

Date	Year group/KS	Area of activity	Lesson in unit	Time	Working area	No. girls/boys	Equipment used

Intended learning outcomes		
By the end of this lesson pupils will be able to:		
NUMBER	STRAND	

LESSON OBSERVATION

Time	Which ILOs are being addressed?	What whole-class learning activities are taking place?	How are the activities differentiated for groups/individuals?	What learning points are being emphasised?	How are equipment and resources organised and pupils managed?	What teaching and learning strategies are being used? What types of learners do these cater for?

Time

Time allocated gives a picture of how pace in the lesson is established. Writing down the time allocation given to each activity/part of the lesson helps you see the balance that the teacher is able to achieve for each activity/part and in particular the amount of time pupils are active.

ILOs being addressed

By identifying the particular ILO that is being addressed with an activity/series of activities, you can trace the progress of the ILOs through the lesson.

Whole-class activities

The teacher's explanations of the tasks pupils are to perform provide the bulk of this section. You may need to note more than one task if the teacher is differentiating by task (see Chapter 11).

Differentiating activities for groups and individuals

Issues related to maximising the achievement of all pupils are covered in Chapter 12, in particular, inclusive teaching in which effective learning opportunities are provided for all pupils. You should note down any pupil/s for whom the task was adapted.

Learning points

Learning points are sometimes referred to as teaching points. Again, adopt the terminology that your own training institution uses. You can complete this section by listening to the points that the teacher asks the pupils to consider. The teacher may identify different learning points depending on the ability of the pupils. Note the techniques, such as demonstrations, that the teacher uses to reinforce these points and also particular words the teacher uses during this interaction. Note also the nature of the learning points for different strands, for example any differences in the type of language used for teaching an E&I strand compared to A&D. Consider how the learning points are delivered to ensure that there is depth in pupil learning, i.e. the 'why' as well as the 'what' and 'how' of the particular aspect of learning.

Management of pupils and organisation of equipment and resources

If you are observing a lesson late in the term/year the teacher will have created a number of rituals and routines in order to streamline the management of pupils and equipment. Try to identify the hidden procedures which have become implicit within the lesson. This includes how to move into and out of activities as well as the organisation of the activity itself, i.e. the organisation of transition phases in the lesson. The teacher may also use learning resources such as work cards. You should look in particular at how the teacher sets up these tasks and the instructions given to pupils for their use.

Teaching and learning strategies

Make a note of particular identifiable teaching strategies the teacher uses. This may be a range of different question and answer techniques to illicit pupil response or to monitor the quality of pupils' learning. The strategy may involve the use of a demonstration to aid performance analysis and the development of pupils' ability to E&I. Note how the strategies used cater for a range of different preferred learning styles (VAK). It is possible that you will be able to see a relationship between the ILO the teacher is working towards and the teaching strategy considered most appropriate.

From recording what happens in the lesson, you should have been able to identify the important aspects of planning which, although not specifically noted in a plan by an experienced teacher, are necessary for you as a beginning teacher to note in detail (see Activities 6.10 and 6.11).

Activity 6.10 Important aspects of planning

Discuss the lesson with the teacher as soon as possible, focusing on the information you have collected. Examples of questions to act as prompts are detailed here. The important point is that you question and ask for clarification on any aspect that you feel would help develop your ability to plan a lesson.

Post-lesson observation interview	
Aspect of the lesson	Suggested questions
Time	What informed the amount of time you spent on each of the learning activities? Did you adjust the timing of any activities? Why was this?
ILOs being addressed	How did you utilise your ILOs during the lesson to support pupil learning? How did your ILOs address different NCPE strands? Did you deliberately adapt any of your ILOs during the lesson? Would you want to revisit any of the ILOs next lesson? Why?
Whole-class activities	What informed the structure of your learning activities? Were they in that order for a particular reason? If you were to teach this lesson again would you alter the learning activities you selected? Why?
Differentiating activities for groups and individuals	How did you identify any pupils during the lesson who you thought needed to have tasks adapted for them? What particular techniques/approaches did you use to differentiate for these pupils?
Learning points	What informed your decision to deliver your learning points at certain key phases of the lesson? Did you use certain strategies when delivering your learning points? How do you use language yourself to develop pupils understanding?
Organisation of equipment and resources and pupil management	What informed the ways in which you organised the equipment and facilities for your lesson? Did you group the pupils in a particular way for different activities? Why? What management strategies did you use to maximise pupil activity time and learning?
Teaching and learning strategies	Did you utilise certain strategies to cater for different preferred learning styles? What were these? How did you structure your use of question and answer throughout the lesson? Why did you select certain pupils to demonstrate?

Activity 6.11 Planning a lesson for an identified area of activity and group of pupils

Using the lesson plan on p. 69 or the proforma on the website (http://www.routledge.com/textbooks/0415361117), or one from your own institution, plan the next lesson to follow on from the one you have observed. In order to do this you need to do the following:

- Obtain a copy of the unit of work from which the lesson is taken.
- Discuss with the class teacher the ILOs for the next lesson, based on the outcomes from your discussion (see Activity 6.10).

SUMMARY

Unit of work and lesson planning demands considerable time and effort. Without clear goals in terms of what you intend the pupils know, do and understand by the end of a unit or lesson, there is a danger that crucial aspects of learning will either not take place or will result in wasted time due to lack of focus. This chapter has tried to show the importance of thinking through all the stages of the planning process. When you sit down to plan a lesson you will have a lot of questions floating around in your head, such as: What am I trying to achieve? What activities do I include in the time I have? How will I differentiate the activities? How will I get the equipment out? etc. By writing the answers to such questions in a systematic way you will be able to 'imagine' yourself in the teaching situation and 'rehearse' the lesson in advance. By doing so, you can anticipate problems that may arise. Over time with a class, you develop routines, rituals and relationships that allow you to predict with more certainty the impact of your decisions on pupil learning.

As you progress as a teacher you find that many aspects of planning become routine and do not need to be written in great detail. You will also find that you are able to adapt your lesson plan as a result of formative assessments you make during the lesson. This confidence in being able to respond to pupils as the lesson unfolds is something that develops gradually. It is, therefore, important that during your ITE you build strong foundations from which you can eventually develop this flexibility.

FURTHER READING

Baumann, A., Bloomfield, A. and Roughton, L. (1997) *Becoming a Secondary School Teacher*, London: Hodder and Stoughton.
Cohen, L., Manion, L. and Morrison, K. (2004) *A Guide to Teaching Practice*, 3rd edn, London: Routledge.
Pollard, A. and Triggs, P. (1997) *Reflective Teaching in the Secondary School*, London: Cassell.
http://www.standards.dfes.gov.uk/schemes2/Secondary_PE This website contains some curriculum planning guidance and exemplar schemes and units of work which are intended to act as a planning resource for physical education teachers in school.

LESSON PLAN

DATE	YEAR GROUP/KS	AREA OF ACTIVITY	LESSON IN UNIT	TIME	WORKING AREA	NO. GIRLS/BOYS	EQUIPMENT REQUIRED

ACTION POINTS FROM ASSESSMENT OF WHOLE CLASS LEARNING LAST LESSON

STRAND	
	KEY WORDS FOR THIS WEEK'S ILOS – REFER TO LAST WEEK'S ASSESSMENT DATA AND USE THESE TO INFORM YOUR ILOs IN THE SECTION BELOW AND YOUR LEARNING POINTS INSIDE PLAN

ACTION POINTS FROM ASSESSMENT OF SAMPLE OF PUPILS' LEARNING LAST LESSON

NAME OF PUPIL	
	DIFFERENTIATION REQUIRED FOR THIS LESSON – REFER TO LAST WEEK'S ASSESSMENT DATA AND USE TO INFORM DIFFERENTIATING LEARNING ACTIVITIES COLUMN INSIDE PLAN

SPECIFIC AND ASSESSABLE INTENDED LEARNING OUTCOMES – CROSS-REFERENCE THESE TO YOUR UNIT ILOS, NUMBER AND ANNOTATE AGAINST THE NATIONAL CURRICULUM PHYSICAL EDUCATION (NCPE) STRANDS AND WRITE AS 'VERB, CONTEXT, QUALITY'

By the end of this lesson pupils will be able to :

NUMBER	STRAND

ASSESSMENT OF WHOLE-CLASS LEARNING

ILO NO. AND STRAND									
KEY WORDS FROM THIS LESSON'S ILOs									
ASSESSMENT OF WHOLE-CLASS LEARNING USING ABOVE KEY WORDS FROM THIS LESSON'S ILOS AND TPS									
	WT	ACH	WB	WT	ACH	WB	WT	ACH	WB
APPROX % OF PUPILS									
KEY WORDS FOR NEXT LESSON'S ILOS									

ASSESSMENT OF LEARNING FOR IDENTIFIED SAMPLE OF PUPILS

PUPIL NAME	ILO 1	ILO 2	ILO 3	ASSESSMENT OF PUPIL LEARNING USING IDENTIFIED KEY WORDS FOR THIS LESSON	ACTION POINTS FOR LEARNING NEXT LESSON

EVALUATION OF YOUR LEARNING AGAINST STANDARDS FOR QTS DETAILED ON LESSON DEBRIEF SHEET

Time	ILOs	Whole-class learning activities	Differentiated learning activities

Learning points – ensure these address all NCPE identified in ILOs	Organisation of pupils, equipment and resources	Teaching styles and strategies

Chapter 7

Planning for pupils' learning in broader dimensions of the curriculum 1

Citizenship, social, moral, spiritual, cultural and personal development

ANDREW THEODOULIDES

INTRODUCTION

The current educational climate gives pupils' learning within broader dimensions of the curriculum a curious place within physical education. On one hand, the Education Reform Act (Department of Education and Science (DES, 1988), the Education (Schools) Act (DES, 1992), the National Curriculum for Physical Education (NCPE) (Department for Education and Employment and the Qualifications and Curriculum Authority (DFEE/QCA, 1999), and Citizenship Education all clearly identify the importance of promoting pupils' learning in broader dimensions of the curriculum. However, in practical terms, it is the four strands of the programme of study (acquiring and developing, selecting and applying, evaluating and improving and knowledge of health and fitness), taught through the breadth of study (i.e. the six areas of activity in the NCPE (athletics, dance, games, gymnastics, outdoor and adventurous activities and swimming) that tend to be the focus of teachers' work. Moreover, when assessing pupils' learning, the 'levels of attainment' reflect learning in the four strands. Given this context an assessment-driven curriculum has the potential to marginalise learning outcomes such as those in the broader dimensions of the curriculum.

The work of physical education teachers, however, is not just about delivering the physical education curriculum. All teachers have a responsibility to promote pupils' wider learning (see Zwozdiak-Myers, *et al.*, 2004). Thus, if aspects of the broader curriculum are to be learned (or developed) through physical education, they must be given appropriate recognition within your work. This chapter explores how you might effectively promote pupils' learning in broader dimensions of the physical education curriculum – specifically in personal, spiritual, moral, social and cultural development and citizenship.

By the end of this chapter you should be able to:

- reflect on your responsibility in teaching broader dimensions of the physical education curriculum;
- explore specific teaching and learning strategies that could be used to effectively promote pupils' learning in these areas.

DEVELOPING A CLEAR COMMITMENT TO PROMOTE PUPILS' LEARNING IN THE BROADER DIMENSIONS OF THE CURRICULUM

There still seems to be a perception by some people that pupils' learning in elements of the broader curriculum are *caught*, that is, learning takes place as an inevitable consequence of taking part (Theodoulides, 2003). But to what extent is this justified? It would be similar to giving pupils a tennis racquet each, a couple of tennis balls and telling them to 'go onto the tennis courts and play tennis'. During the lesson you do not modify the game to make it easier for the pupils to learn the skills and techniques of tennis, nor do you give them any feedback on how to hit shots correctly. In effect the pupils just play tennis. Activity 7.1 identifies the focus for pupils' learning, while Activity 7.2 develops a reflective approach.

Activity 7.1 Developing a focus for pupils' learning in broader dimensions of the PE curriculum

1   In a lesson you are going to teach, write a learning outcome that relates to one of the broader dimensions of the physical education curriculum. For example,

- Pupils understand that they have a moral responsibility towards the safety of others when providing support in gymnastics.
- Pupils are able to reflect upon the sense of well-being swimming can bring to the quality of their lives.
- Pupils are able to consider the needs of others when making decisions whilst in the role of a group leader.

Learning outcome

How could you differentiate this outcome (see Chapter 12)?
Most pupils should be able to:

Some pupils will not have made as much progress and will be able to:

A few pupils will have progressed further and will be able to:

What range of teaching and learning strategies could you use in order to meet these outcomes?

Now teach the lesson.

2   At the end of the lesson reflect upon how successful you were in helping the pupils to meet the learning outcomes.

- To what extent were they achieved?
- Were the learning activities appropriate?
- How easy was it to promote pupils' learning in this area?
- How did the pupils react to what you did?
- What would you do differently next time?
- Use this information to inform the planning of your next lesson.

> **Activity 7.2** Developing a reflective approach to the teaching of broader dimensions of the curriculum within physical education
>
> 1 In the tennis example on pp. 73–74, what criticisms would you make about your 'teaching'?
> 2 What is the likely outcome of your 'teaching' in terms of pupils' learning of the skills and techniques of tennis?
> 3 Compare this with pupils' learning in the broader dimensions of the curriculum. How does pupils' learning in these areas differ from the example given above, if at all?
> 4 In your experience, to what extent do physical education teachers teach pupils about broader dimensions of the curriculum or do they assume 'it just happens'?

In doing Activity 7.3 you may well have realised that without a range of effective teaching and learning strategies, a teacher has very little control over what pupils learn. Your pupils may well develop into excellent tennis players, who are technically very good and who know how and when to hit the right shot. But equally, they may pick up some bad habits resulting in poor technique. It would be unacceptable for a teacher to adopt a teaching approach in which pupils were given a racquet and ball and told to 'go away and play' in the hope that they will learn simply by taking part. Yet, this is how many teachers approach pupils' learning in the broader dimensions of the curriculum. The perceived validity of this *laissez-faire* teaching approach in one sense provides a means for teachers to teach with the minimum of effort. Consequently they see no reason to adopt any specific teaching and learning strategies to promote pupils' learning. However, this is not educationally sound and for teaching and *learning* to be more effective, teachers should adopt a more critically reflective approach towards the way in which they can promote pupils' learning in broader dimensions of the curriculum too. If you do not take a proactive role in promoting pupils' learning in this domain, then there is no guarantee of the type and level of learning that will take place. A good starting point is to identify where units of work have the potential to promote pupils' learning in dimensions of the broader curriculum (see Zwozdiak-Myers *et al.*, 2004).

> **Activity 7.3** Matching the teacher's intentions to pupils' learning
>
> Observe a lesson taught by an experienced teacher and answer the following questions:
>
> • Where in the lesson do you think pupils' learning in one (or more) dimensions of the broader curriculum may have developed?
> • After observing, state *specifically* what you thought the pupils learnt in dimensions of the broader curriculum.
> • Ask three pupils what they think that they learned in the broader curriculum dimension. What did they say?
> • Now ask the teacher what s/he thinks the pupils learned. What did s/he say?
> • Do these match up?

IDENTIFYING PUPILS' LEARNING IN BROADER DIMENSIONS OF THE CURRICULUM

When opportunities to develop pupils' learning in broader dimensions of the physical education curriculum are identified, the learning outcomes must support other learning that is taking place within the unit of work and not be a 'bolt-on-extra', included 'just for the sake of it'. If learning in the broader dimensions of the curriculum is not seen to be *integral* to the work of the unit (by both teachers and pupils), its value is immediately diminished (see Activity 7.4).

Activity 7.4 Planning for pupils' learning

Look through the units of work that you are going to teach. Where in these units is there a *specific* contribution to pupils' learning in broader dimensions of the curriculum?

Identify further opportunities to include specific unit learning outcomes which relate to broader dimensions of the curriculum. Bear in mind that learning in one dimension of the broader curriculum may overlap into another. For example, being a leader (personal development) requires pupils to communicate with others (social development) and to show consideration for others (moral development). Where possible, identify teaching and learning activities to meet these outcomes. Dance is shown as an example.

Unit	Learning outcome	Curriculum dimension	Teaching and learning strategies
Dance	*Pupils understand the cultural context of the haka*	*Cultural development*	*Pupils watch a video of the haka and complete a component chart to identify aspects of the dance's symbolism.* *Teacher-led phrase which demonstrates stylistic features and inherent symbolism of the haka.* *Pupils devise their own phrase of movement in the style of haka.* *Pupils explain the symbolism within their phrase.*

DEVELOPING EFFECTIVE TEACHING AND LEARNING STRATEGIES TO PROMOTE PUPILS' LEARNING IN BROADER DIMENSIONS OF THE CURRICULUM

Having identified where breadth of study areas could promote pupils' learning in the broader dimensions of the curriculum, the challenge facing teachers is to write learning outcomes which are clearly focused and develop a range of effective teaching and learning strategies which enable pupils to achieve them. Two features are important here.

First, you should clearly explain to pupils that they are engaged in activities that promote learning in broader dimensions of the curriculum. For example, from a 'fair play' perspective, if your intention is for pupils 'to respect the decision of the referee' (social and moral learning), then the games must each have a referee. However, it is also important to inform pupils of the reasons for such activities. A game may have a referee for other (practical) reasons (e.g. because you cannot referee all the games at once), which are not related to developing pupils' learning in the social and moral domain. You should not assume that pupils will be aware of your intentions if these are not made explicit. A good starting point might be for you to ask questions which engage pupils in discussion of the need for referees in games and why it is morally necessary to respect their decisions. Useful opening questions could be: 'Was the referee effective?', 'Did s/he make any mistakes?', 'Were these deliberate?', 'How should you act when a referee makes a mistake?', 'Why should we respect referees?', 'Why should we respect other people?'

Second, part of the lesson must include investigation, discussion, practice, or other such learning strategies, which directly promote pupils' learning in *that* specific area of the broader dimensions of the curriculum (see Whitehead and Zwozdiak-Myers, 2004). For example, if the intention is to promote pupils' social skills by expecting them to work in groups in dance in order to discuss compositional ideas, then pupils ought to receive feedback on what constitutes effective co-operation in the *social context*. Thus, feedback would be specific to social skills, not compositional ideas. In this context, the teacher might focus on how effective pupils were in, e.g. articulating their own ideas; listening to the ideas of other pupils or other such (social) interactions (see Activity 7.5).

Activity 7.5 Developing effective teaching and learning strategies

List as many different tasks as you can think of that would promote pupils' understanding of 'fair play' in team games.

- How would you structure these tasks?
- What *progressions* would you use to increase pupils' learning about 'fair play'?
- What *crucial* points would you expect pupils to have learnt by the end of the last task?

REACTING TO OPPORTUNITIES WHICH PROMOTE PUPILS' LEARNING IN BROADER DIMENSIONS OF THE CURRICULUM

Although it is incumbent upon teachers to plan for pupils' learning in the broader dimensions of the curriculum, opportunities sometimes arise that are not planned for. In these situations teachers use their knowledge and professional judgement as to how and when such opportunities need to be utilised effectively if they are to promote pupils' learning.

Read Activity 7.6a. Despite the teacher's good intentions, as a learning experience it is unlikely that the strategy he employed furthered pupils' understanding. Let us examine the

Activity 7.6a Engaging pupils' learning

Consider the example below which could be typical of the kind of incident that occurs in games lessons.

The pupils are playing a small-sided game of rugby near the end of their lesson. As the game progresses, some pupils start appealing to the referee for him to make a decision in their favour. 'Ref, our ball!' says one boy after the ball goes off the pitch. This happens with increasing frequency. The teacher stops the game and addresses the group. He says, 'In football you may shout and appeal for the ball, but in rugby we don't do that.' He restarts the game and the boys carry on playing. However, a few minutes later another pupil appeals to the teacher for a decision. As the game continues the teacher says to the boy, 'Right, Patrick, off you go run around the rugby pitch. I told you not to appeal!' The bemused pupil leaves the game and starts running around the rugby pitch as a punishment. A little later another pupil appeals for the ball. Again the teacher tells the pupil, 'Go on, off you go around the pitch. I told you no appealing. I told you it might be all right in some sports, but not in rugby.'

1   What do you think the teacher wanted the pupils to understand in this incident?

2   Is the strategy the teacher adopted conducive to promoting understanding and appreciation of the relevant issues? Give reasons.

incident. Correctly, the teacher has reacted to the way in which some pupils challenged the referee's decisions. Clearly he believed that he was teaching the pupils something about the way in which rugby ought to be played; that is, the way in which players should respect the referee's decisions (a moral issue). However it is not clear whether pupils recognised the moral implications of their behaviour and knew why their responses were wrong. Likewise it seems unlikely that any pupil, simply because s/he is sent to run around a field, or the other pupils who continued with the game, would make the desired moral connections (an example of how, if learning is left to be 'caught', there is no guarantee of what will be learned). Even if there was no more appealing to the referee for the ball, it cannot be claimed that this demonstrated an improvement in moral action, given pupils' lack of moral reflection. Therefore for pupils to understand the moral implications of their/other pupils' actions the teacher should engage them briefly in some discussion (at least) and reflection about what is, or is not, acceptable behaviour within team games.

You also need to recognise that it is undesirable for teachers to give pupils a punishment (in this case running around the playing field) which is related to the type of activity pupils are engaged in as part of their lesson. If teachers are to foster pupils' enthusiasm for learning, this strategy is inappropriate. Hence, examples such as 'running around the field,' or 'doing ten press-ups' fuel pupils' dislike of physical activity rather than encourage them to take part (see Activity 7.6b).

Activity 7.6b Adopting a different approach to teaching a moral dimension

1   How would you have handled this situation?
2   What would you want the pupils to understand/learn about appealing to the referee for the ball in rugby?
3   Is the teacher right to tell pupils that appealing to the referee in football is acceptable?
4   What teaching and learning strategies would you have used to meet this learning outcome (see your answer for question 2)?
5   What questions might you have asked pupils?
6   How would you know if your teaching of this learning outcome had been successful?

SUMMARY

This chapter has highlighted how physical education teachers can be effective in promoting pupils' learning in the broader dimensions of the curriculum. It is not sufficient to claim that it 'just happens', there should be a clear commitment by teachers to promote pupils' learning in this area – as shown in their teaching of physical education itself. Therefore clearly planned learning outcomes which relate to the broader dimensions of the curriculum should feature in all units of work and lesson plans, supported by teaching and learning strategies which engage pupils in reflecting upon and learning about their own (and others') behaviour, values and attitudes within and beyond physical education.

FURTHER READING

Beedy, J. P. (1997) *Sports Plus: Positive Learning Using Sports*, Hamilton: Project Adventure. In this book the author highlights teaching and learning strategies teachers might use to promote pupils' learning in aspects of personal, social and moral development within sport. These 'teachable moments' provide teachers with ideas for engaging pupils in learning experiences that relate to broader dimensions of the curriculum.

Laker, A. (2001) *Developing Personal, Social and Moral Education Through Physical Education*, London: RoutledgeFalmer. This book contains a detailed analysis of the wider issues surrounding the way in which learning in the broader dimensions of the curriculum is conceptualised within education and more specifically within PE. The book also contains some practical guidance on how to approach the planning and delivery of outcomes in this wider domain.

Chapter 8 Planning for pupils' learning in broader dimensions of the curriculum 2

Key skills and the use of information and communications technology

RICHARD BLAIR

INTRODUCTION

The learning needs of the pupils we teach are constantly changing. As teachers we have a responsibility to ensure that our pupils have the necessary skills and competencies to achieve independence upon leaving school and entering the workplace and adult life in the twenty-first century.

Chapter 7 looked at some of the responsibilities of the physical education teacher beyond those directly related to the physical education curriculum – specifically promoting the development of social, moral, spiritual, cultural and citizenship elements of the curriculum. This chapter looks at promoting pupils' learning in physical education in two other areas of broader dimensions – key skills and the use of information and communications technology (ICT) in physical education. Together these two chapters should enable you to consider the broader curriculum in your planning.

By the end of this chapter you should be able to:

* understand the teacher's responsibility regarding the development of pupils' key skills;
* plan lessons with explicit opportunities for pupils to develop key skills;
* understand the role of ICT to enhance learning.

WHAT ARE KEY SKILLS?

> Key skills are a range of essential skills that underpin success in education, employment, lifelong learning and personal development.
>
> (DfES, 2005)

Abbott and Ryan (2000) identified that in order to meet the needs of the economy people need the following:

* the mastery of basic skills;
* the ability to work with others;
* the ability to deal with constant distractions;
* the ability to work at various levels within an organisation;
* to be able to use verbal skills;
* to be able to engage in problem solving and decision-making.

Now complete Activity 8.1.

Activity 8.1   What key skills and competencies will pupils need when they start work?

Think about the key skills and competencies that will be needed by each person when they start work:

- a 16-year-old school leaver looking for work as a leisure assistant at a local leisure centre;
- a 19-year-old school leaver looking for work as a trainee sports development officer for a local authority;
- a 22-year-old Physical Education graduate starting their NQT year.

Are there any similarities in the skills and competencies needed by these three people as they are about to start work? What are they?

Which of the skills identified by Abbott and Ryan (2000) are needed by each of these three people?

In schools six key skills are identified which should be taught across all subjects in the National Curriculum, including physical education (www.nc.uk.net). These are:

- Communication
- Application of number
- Working with others
- Improving own learning and performance
- Problem solving
- Information Technology.

These key skills need to be 'mapped' into the curriculum (see Activity 8.2). The scope of each of these key skills and how they can be planned for in physical education are outlined below.

Activity 8.2   Planning to include key skills in your lessons

Reflect on a lesson plan that you have already taught. If possible, select a lesson in which you were observed teaching.

- Did you explicitly plan to include any of the skills identified by Abbott and Ryan (2000) in your lesson?
- Is there any reference through your planning or the lesson assessment/ evaluation of pupil learning that they have developed any of these skills?
- Where could you have included development of any of the above skills within your lesson?

Communication

The key communication skills of speaking, listening, reading and writing can all be incorporated into lessons, although in physical education there has traditionally been a natural bias towards speaking and listening. When talking to other pupils or the teacher, pupils should be taught to express themselves correctly and appropriately. This can be achieved through all six areas of activity and in different ways, e.g. pupils may be asked to talk about how they are planning their own performance; they may be asked to evaluate their own or others' work; or they may be asked to give feedback on other pupils' work. Feedback should always take place against predetermined success criteria. These criteria are best written on cards, developed by the teacher, pupils, or commercially produced, and should help develop reading skills. Pupils should also be taught the technical and specialist vocabulary of physical education and how to use and spell these words. They should also learn to listen to other people – including listening to instructions and to feedback, from the teacher or another pupil.

There are other opportunities for reading and writing to be incorporated into physical education lessons – particularly in GCSE and A Level classes. Although these can be incorporated at Key Stage 3, it is important that they do not detract from time pupils spend on physical activity itself.

Application of number

In physical education the interpretation of numerical information can be achieved through all six areas of activity. One obvious example is athletics where pupils' skills in developing mental calculation and their ability to interpret the results and present the findings can be developed. Other examples include using maps in Outdoor and Adventurous Activities (OAA) or producing diagrams/patterns of work in gymnastics, dance and games. The application of number in all activities is also aided through the use of ICT such as stopwatches, laptops and digital cameras.

Working with others

The nature of many physical education activities lends itself to pupils working together in a collaborative environment with other pupils to meet a challenge. There are many opportunities for these skills to be explicitly planned for in all six areas of activity. OAA, for example, lends itself to pupils having to work as a team, for example, to make their way up a course without touching the ground. Similarly, pupils may choreograph a group dance or a pair sequence in gymnastics.

Improving own learning and performance

The key skill of improving own learning and performance involves pupils reflecting on and critically evaluating their work, what they have learnt and identifying ways to improve their learning and performance. The latter is at the very heart of the 'evaluating and improving performance' strand of the National Curriculum for Physical Education. You should constantly provide pupils with opportunities to review their work and discuss ways to improve their learning.

Problem solving

Physical education is full of potential for pupils to develop skills and strategies to solve problems in a variety of contexts. Included in this are the skills of identifying and understanding a problem, planning ways to solve a problem, monitoring progress in tackling a problem and reviewing solutions to problems. For example, in games you could set up a small-sided game and state that the challenge or problem for the pupils to solve is how to get the ball to the line without making a forward pass. This involves the pupils working as a team to solve the problem. However, as with all other aspects of the broader curriculum, it is important that you plan for these specifically in both units of work and lessons.

Table 8.1 provides examples of how the range of key skills can be explicitly developed in the area of games. You should add your own examples to each of these.

Table 8.1 Key skills in games

Key skill	Examples	Activities
Communication	Speaking, listening, expressing an opinion, debating and discussing. Reading and writing. Forms of non-verbal communication.	Work as a pair/team to solve a problem and communicate ideas. During a doubles badminton game talk to your partner and plan strategy for future success Giving and receiving feedback, e.g. an observer during a badminton game gives feedback against predetermined success criteria.
Application of number	Collecting and analysing data, measuring, calculating.	Scoring in striking and fielding games. Different shots are worth a different amount of points. Invasion games using number to help pupils find and work out the angles of support and the percentage chance of the ball arriving at its intended destination.
Working with others	Whole and small group discussion, teamwork to achieve a set challenge	Invasion games: working as a team to solve a set problem or challenge. Net and wall games: working as a pair in badminton or tennis to strategically plan how to outscore opponents.
Improving own learning and performance	Evaluating, making, judgements, target setting, practising, persevering, recognising improvements.	In an invasion games lesson pupils work with the teacher to create success criteria against which they can be assessed. Pupils record evidence of their performance (possibly through the use of ICT (e.g. digital camera)) and then using the success criteria evaluate and make judgements that help them to improve their performance. This should be supported and reinforced by feedback from the teacher or other pupils that identifies and builds on progress and improvement.
Problem solving	Reasoning, divergent thinking, using imagination, creativity, applying principles, breaking problems down into component parts, using a variety of approaches to solve a problem.	All games are problems to be solved and can be conditioned to present specific problems to achieve particular ends. For example, teaching passing through a practice or game that sets a problem of having to pass the ball to be successful. The teacher may set the pupils the challenge of, for example, if they score a goal they get one point, however, if they make 3 passes they get 3 points.

For each of the key skills above think of other examples (see Activity 8.3). As you can see, many of these activities enable several key skills to be addressed at the same time.

Having identified and planned where in a unit of work and individual lessons you can include selected key skills, it is important that you plan carefully how you will create specific and assessable learning outcomes to measure pupil learning.

It is also important to remember that you need to plan for pupils' development in the key skills over a longer period of time, for example, through a scheme of work or Key Stage (see Activity 8.4).

Activity 8.3 Developing key skills in your teaching

Using the example provided for games activities in Table 8.1, outline ways in which the key skills could be taught in each of the five remaining areas of activity; gymnastics, swimming, dance, athletics or OAA.

Area of activity . . . .

Key skill	Examples	Activities
Communication	Speaking, listening, expressing an opinion, debating and discussing, reading and writing, forms of non-verbal communication.	
Application of number	Collecting and analysing data, measuring, calculating.	
Working with others	Whole and small group discussion, teamwork to achieve a set challenge.	
Improving own learning and performance	Evaluating, making, judgements, target setting, practising, persevering, recognising improvements.	
Problem solving	Reasoning, divergent thinking, using imagination, creativity, applying principles, breaking problems down into component parts, using a variety of approaches to solve a problem.	

Using the information in Table 8.1 and Activity 8.3, write learning outcomes and associated activities that promote the development of key skills in a selected activity. Try this both with an activity in which you are very confident and one which you have less confidence to teach. An example for gymnastics is provided below.

Key skill	Learning outcome: By the end of this lesson pupils will be able to:	Learning points
Communication	*Provide feedback to a partner on the quality of his/her sequence, using criteria provided by the teacher*	• *Speak clearly* • *Use appropriate terminology e.g. body tension and quality of body shape*

USING ICT IN PHYSICAL EDUCATION

ICT is included as one of the key skills which should permeate the curriculum. It is given special consideration here since there has been a significant drive by the government to raise pupils' achievement through the use of ICT across all subject areas.

The use of ICT as a tool to analyse and record a physical performance has a powerful effect on pupils' motivation and achievement. Whether it is using a digital or video camera for physical images or a stopwatch to record times – ICT can provide much-needed evidence of knowledge of performance or knowledge of results or both. It would be of great advantage if every physical education teacher in particular had a digital video camera to record performance and achievement (see Activity 8.5).

Activity 8.5 Using ICT in your teaching

Answer the following questions – using examples from as many areas of activity as you can:

- In what ways can ICT enhance pupil learning within physical education?
- What are the possible challenges as ICT is introduced into physical education?

The question that you must ask yourself when making a decision to use ICT is, do the organisation and use of ICT in this lesson, with this group of pupils, through this area of activity, at this particular time of the day, at this stage of the unit, etc. support and promote the learning of the pupils? Furthermore, does it help teachers and pupils to assess work formatively and provide sufficient and specific feedback to improve pupils' performance/attainment/achievement? Activity 8.6 helps you to decide how to use ICT in one of your lessons.

Activity 8.6 Using ICT in one of your lessons

When deciding whether or not to use ICT in one of your lessons, answer the following questions. Make your decision on the basis of your responses.

- Why is ICT being used?
- What are you going to use it for?
- Will ICT improve pupils' skills, knowledge and understanding in relation to the strands? In what contexts?
- Will it develop pupils' knowledge and understanding of the activity?
- How is its use going to be integrated into teaching and learning in the activity?
- Thus, what added value does it bring to the learning experience?
- Does it allow teachers and pupils to assess work formatively by enabling pupils to review, evaluate and improve their own and others' performance and provide sufficient and specific feedback to improve pupils' performance/attainment/achievement?
- Therefore, is the use of ICT appropriate for this group of pupils, to achieve learning outcomes in these strands, through this area of activity, at this particular time of day and at this stage of the unit, etc.? Does it support and promote the learning of the pupils?

If the answer to these questions is yes, then it is appropriate to use ICT, if not, it is not appropriate.

One of the challenges you face is access to equipment or resources. This can be at a range of different levels, including access to cameras, laptops, projectors, stopwatches, etc. It can also include resources that support the use of the original resource. For example, if pupils in a GCSE class have been given homework to produce a Powerpoint presentation, there would need to be a projector and screen available to present the work to create the maximum learning opportunity.

It is at this second stage of the process that more complications can arise. It is important that the information collected is used as evidence of performance and achievement/ attainment and to provide feedback on pupils' performance. In order for the pictorial, video or numerical evidence to be used to aid pupils' learning, it is vital that there is access to facilities to edit or interpret the evidence or data. There are a number of packages available that allow digital images to be manipulated. Access to these facilities is one problem, but another is knowledge and skills to be able to edit and interpret effectively (see Activity 8.7).

Activity 8.7   ICT available to support your teaching

Complete the chart below in relation to the following three points:

1   Undertake an audit of the ICT equipment available to the physical education department in your school. In column 1 identify each piece of equipment separately.
2   In column 2 record how the equipment is currently used.
3   In column 3 identify how the equipment could be used further to enhance pupil learning.

Description of equipment	Current use	Potential use

ICT should therefore be used where appropriate to enhance pupil learning. However, it should only be used in order to support pupils in developing their knowledge, skills and understanding of being physically educated (or to develop broader skills outlined in the unit of work). It is also important that it does not detract from the time in which pupils are engaged in physical activity. It may be appropriate for data collected in physical education to be analysed or interpreted in another lesson, e.g. for heart rates to be analysed in biology/science.

Note of caution: if you are using ICT to create digital images, it is important that you are aware of and consider data protection. At present, there is little advice for teachers, which raises questions regarding permission from parents. Good practice suggests that where pupils' images are likely to be recorded, you should seek parental permission prior to the lesson. For further information on this, visit www.hants.gov.uk/TC/cg/photoschools.html

SUMMARY

The six key skills are key aspects of pupil learning across the curriculum. These key skills are embedded in the National Curriculum because they help learners to improve their learning and performance in education, employment, lifelong learning and personal development. As we have seen, physical education is ideally placed to make a valuable contribution to the development of pupils' key skills and many of them are already being met through teachers' good practice. As with other aspects of the broader curriculum, however, this should not be left to chance but should permeate progressively as planned learning for all pupils.

FURTHER READING

Abbott, J. and Ryan, T. (2000) *The Unfinished Revolution: Learning, Human Behaviour, Community and Political Paradox*, Stafford: Network Educational Press Ltd.

Bentley, T. and Gardner, H. (1998) *Learning Beyond the Classroom: Education for a Changing World*, London: RoutledgeFalmer.

Stidder, G. (2004) The use of informational and communications technology (ICT) in PE, in S. Capel (ed.) *Learning to Teach Physical Education in the Secondary School: A Companion to School Experience*, 2nd edn, London: RoutledgeFalmer, pp. 219–38. Although the first readings are generic, the chapter by Stidder looks at the rationale for using ICT in physical education, its use across the areas of activity and in the four strands as well as in assessment, recording and reporting, examination work, including non-participants in physical education and cross-curricular work. It also looks at the use of ICT in the administration of a physical education department – including for planning, recording pupil information, supporting extra-curricular activity and promoting physical education in the school. It contains a very useful section on some of the resources available.

http://www.nc.uk.net

www.hants.gov.uk/TC/cg/photoschools.html

Part 3   Teaching lessons

Chapter 9   Creating an effective learning environment which promotes 'behaviour for learning'

SUSAN CAPEL AND JULIA LAWRENCE

INTRODUCTION

The nature of physical education is such that there is tremendous potential for your lessons to be ruined by poor organisation and management. This has a detrimental effect on your confidence, but more importantly on the quality of pupils' learning. Good organisation and management are therefore paramount if you are to develop an environment in which all pupils can learn effectively. A positive lesson climate provides the most effective learning environment. This is consistent with and supports a positive or preventative approach to behaviour management in which pupils have a key role to play. This approach is called 'behaviour for learning' (see Garner, 2005, for more information). This approach is consistent with an inclusive schooling approach (see Chapter 11).

Your ability to organise, manage and develop a positive learning climate to support a 'behaviour for learning' approach develops over a period of time as you gain experience. Do not expect to have 'perfected' your skills during your initial teacher education (ITE). What is important is that you adopt a reflective approach so that you can identify your own strengths and areas for development and set yourself specific targets for development.

By the end of this chapter you should understand and be able to adopt strategies in your teaching to:

- organise and manage your lessons to maximise the time you spend promoting learning;
- establish and develop an effective learning environment;
- develop a positive lesson climate which supports a 'behaviour for learning' approach to pupil behaviour.

ORGANISING AND MANAGING A LESSON

Organisation and management of lessons can be daunting and is likely to be one of your major foci early in your school experience. As with all other aspects of your teaching and the promotion of pupil learning, it is essential that you do not leave organisation and management to chance but that you plan it. It is helpful to view organisation from the point of view of pupils. This helps you to clarify the message you wish to give; which you must then deliver consistently and through as many routes as possible.

Good organisation and management in themselves do not promote pupils' learning; rather, they enable you to establish an effective learning environment which allows pupils to spend more time on-task engaged in learning activities. It is also worth noting that pupils are often more disruptive and more behavioural problems occur, when they are not on-task (see Activities 9.1, 9.2).

Activity 9.1   Planning the organisation and management of lessons

In column 2 list strategies that may be employed to ensure that each of the organisation and management tasks in column 1 is completed effectively and efficiently to maximise the time available for pupil learning. You may also complete column 2 in relation to your own teaching by identifying the strategy in column 2 and asking someone to record in column 3 the time the strategies you use take. How does this impact on pupils' learning time? Adapt/change the strategies in light of your own evaluations/observations, feedback from pupils' responses in the lesson and from the observer.

Task	Possible strategies	Time strategy takes in the lesson
How are pupils let into the changing room?		
When and how are valuables and jewellery collected?		
When and how is the register taken?		
Equipment/resources, e.g. Where is equipment going to be located during the lesson? Who is responsible for getting it out/putting it away? How is this going to be organised?		
Organisation of activities and movement between them, e.g. how is the first activity arranged and how is the change from one activity to the next managed?		
Organisation of groupings, e.g. how are pupils assigned to groups? Do groups change during the lesson? If so, how is this managed?		

You may want to repeat this activity using other organisational and management activities, before, during and after the lesson. See, for example, Lawrence *et al.* (2004: 82–97). You may also observe an experienced teacher and note the differences.

Complete this sheet twice; once on an observation of your teaching completed by a teacher and once by you on an observation of a lesson taken by an experienced teacher. What differences are there in results? Reflect on what the data tells you about your teaching and pupils' learning, then identify how you can increase the time pupils spend actively engaged in learning.

Purpose

This instrument is often used to judge teaching effectiveness in physical education. Specifically, its purpose is to describe the amount of time pupils are engaged in motor activity at an appropriate level of difficulty. This is based on the assumption that the longer pupils are engaged in motor activity at an appropriate level of difficulty, the more they learn.

Definitions of categories

Four categories of activity are identified:

- *Motor appropriate (MA)* The pupil is engaged in a motor activity related to the subject matter in such a way as to produce a high degree of success.
- *Motor inappropriate (MI)* The pupil is engaged in a motor activity related to the subject matter, but the task or activity is either too difficult or too easy for the pupil's capabilities, therefore practising it does not contribute to the achievement of lesson objectives.
- *Motor supporting (MS)* The pupil is engaged in a motor activity related to the subject matter with the purpose of helping others to learn or perform the activity (for example sending balls to others or spotting the trampoline).
- *Not motor engaged (NM)* The pupil is not involved in a motor activity related to the subject matter.

Recording procedures

There are four different methods of observation available to collect ALT-PE data about the categories above. These methods use:

- *Interval recording* This involves alternating observing and recording at short intervals. One pupil or an alternating sample of pupils is used. The observer watches one pupil during the *observing interval*. During the *recording interval*, the observer records the observation as *MA*, *MI*, *MS* or *NM*. Data can be presented as a percentage of each category. This is the most common observation method used.
- *Group time sampling* This involves the observer scanning the group for 15 seconds every 2 minutes, and counting the number of pupils engaged at an appropriate level of motor activity (*MA*). Data can be presented as an average for the class.
- *Duration recording* This involves the observer using a time line to categorise into one of the four categories (*MA*, *MI*, *MS* or *NM*), what one pupil is doing the entire period. Alternatively, the observer can measure *MA* time only. A

stopwatch is started when the pupil is appropriately engaged and stopped when the engagement stops. Total *MA* time for the lesson can be presented as a percentage of total lesson time.
- *Event recording*. This involves the observer counting the number of *MA* practice trials at an appropriate level of difficulty (the practice must include discrete trials). Trials are measured (and data presented) per minute or over longer units of time.

Example of ALT-PE using the interval recording method

To use this method of recording the coding format is divided into *intervals*. In each interval box there are two levels: a top level and a lower level. The top level of the interval box is used to describe the *context of the interval* (*C*). There are ten choices of context from three categories: general content, subject matter knowledge and subject matter motor (see below). This decision is made on the basis of what the class as a whole is doing, for example, are they involved in warm-up, a lecture on strategy, or skill practice?

The lower level of the interval box is used to describe the *involvement of one pupil* (*LI*). Choices are from the categories described as not motor engaged and motor engaged (see below).

The *letter code* for the appropriate category is placed in the appropriate part of the interval box.

Typically, it is suggested that three pupils of differing skill levels are observed, *alternating observation* of them at every interval.

This system provides a total picture of what the class does throughout the lesson and a finely graded picture of the involvement of several pupils.

Those interval boxes marked as motor appropriate (*MA*) are ALT-PE intervals. Total ALT-PE is the total for the pupil during the lesson.
Source: Siedentop *et al.* (1982)

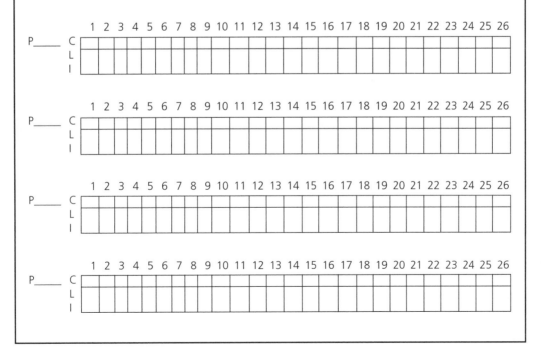

Activity 9.2 *continued*

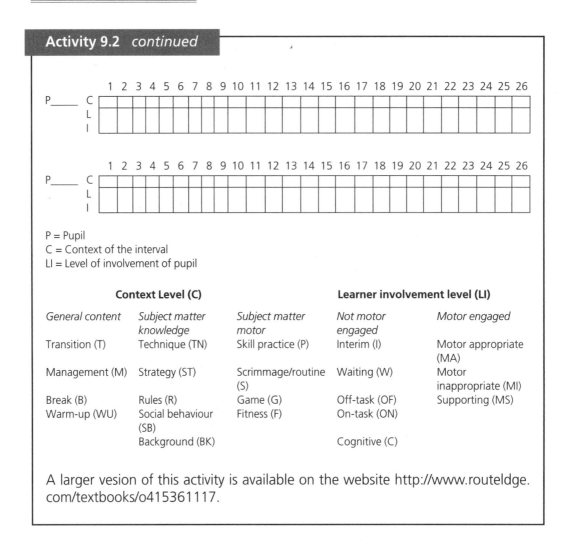

P____ C
     L
     I

1 2 3 4 5 6 7 8 9 10 11 12 13 14 15 16 17 18 19 20 21 22 23 24 25 26

P____ C
     L
     I

1 2 3 4 5 6 7 8 9 10 11 12 13 14 15 16 17 18 19 20 21 22 23 24 25 26

P = Pupil
C = Context of the interval
LI = Level of involvement of pupil

Context Level (C)			**Learner involvement level (LI)**	
General content	*Subject matter knowledge*	*Subject matter motor*	*Not motor engaged*	*Motor engaged*
Transition (T)	Technique (TN)	Skill practice (P)	Interim (I)	Motor appropriate (MA)
Management (M)	Strategy (ST)	Scrimmage/routine (S)	Waiting (W)	Motor inappropriate (MI)
Break (B)	Rules (R)	Game (G)	Off-task (OF)	Supporting (MS)
Warm-up (WU)	Social behaviour (SB)	Fitness (F)	On-task (ON)	
	Background (BK)		Cognitive (C)	

A larger vesion of this activity is available on the website http://www.routeldge.com/textbooks/o415361117.

ESTABLISHING AN EFFECTIVE LEARNING ENVIRONMENT

A positive lesson climate provides the most effective learning environment (Capel *et al*. 2004: 103). Many factors contribute to this climate. Interactions and relationships between teacher and pupils and between pupils are positive and effective. Pupils are placed at the centre of lesson planning and delivery. A positive teaching style is used in which feedback is given for appropriate work; this motivates pupils to learn and enhances their self-esteem. The lesson has a relaxed, but purposeful atmosphere. Pupils are expected to learn and to be on-task, supported by a committed and enthusiastic teacher who is confident, authoritative and clearly in control of the situation, but also caring, understanding and sensitive. The working space is clean and tidy and conveys care and attention to pupils and their learning (see ibid.: 102–19). Establishing an effective learning environment with a positive lesson climate is something that is within your control, so you must consider the factors that contribute to this as an explicit part of your lesson planning, (see Activity 9.3).

An effective learning environment with a positive lesson climate supports a 'behaviour for learning' approach, which is relevant to all pupils. Effective relationships are central to the 'behaviour for learning' approach. The approach emphasises teacher expectations and the value placed on behaving in ways which enable and maximise pupil learning. Targets are set that are reachable (Garner, 2005: 136–7). This approach contrasts with a reactive approach which focuses on behaviours that the teacher does not want and in which pupils are disciplined or punished for poor behaviour *after* it occurs. Indeed, a reactive approach can 'worsen or even create the very problems it is intended to eradicate' (Weare, 2004: 63).

Activity 9.3 An effective learning environment

Observe a lesson and note in column 2 evidence of each aspect of an effective learning environment listed in column 1. In column 3 note how you will develop this in your own teaching.

Aspects of an effective learning environment	Evidence of this aspect	How you will develop this in your own teaching
Positive interaction between teacher and pupils		
Effective interpersonal relationships between teacher and pupils		
Positive relationships between pupils		
Positive teaching style – feedback is given for appropriate work		
Pupils' self-esteem is enhanced		
Pupils are motivated		
Pupils placed at the centre of lesson planning and delivery		
Lesson has relaxed, but purposeful atmosphere		
Pupils are expected to learn and to be on task		
Committed and enthusiastic teacher		
Confident and authoritative teacher		
Teacher clearly in control of the situation		
Caring, understanding and sensitive teacher		
Working space conveys care and attention to pupils and their learning	*e.g. floor clean, apparatus put away, posters on wall are recent, relevant, laminated and not hanging off the wall*	*e.g. ensure that space is tidy before starting lesson and that equipment is put away after it has been used (during and after the lesson)*

DEVELOPING A POSITIVE LESSON CLIMATE WHICH SUPPORTS A 'BEHAVIOUR FOR LEARNING' APPROACH TO PUPIL BEHAVIOUR

A negative or poor lesson climate may result in pupils demonstrating poor, inappropriate or unacceptable behaviour; a continuum of behaviour from 'low level', e.g. talking out of turn, distracting others, occasionally arriving late for class; to more serious, e.g. 'acting out' behaviour, non-attendance, verbal or physical aggression, wilful disobedience, bullying, etc. (DfE, 1994). There are a number of (often overlapping) factors that cause inappropriate behaviour. These include factors relating to the individual, the culture, curriculum, school ethos, relationships, external barriers to participation and learning. More specifically they include, for example, that

- the curriculum is not seen as relevant or is inaccessible;
- tasks are not differentiated sufficiently so some pupils are bored, whereas for others the task is too demanding or the task requires too much effort;
- there is a break in the lesson because of, for example, poor planning resulting in taking too long to organise pupils into groups/teams or getting out equipment;
- equipment failure;
- poor pace to the lesson;
- a breakdown in communication, for example, because of poor instructions;
- peer/group pressure resulting in alienation;
- negative experiences of schooling;
- physiological needs are not met.

Therefore, it is important that you use strategies to prevent inappropriate behaviour before it occurs. Bleach (2000) identified, for example, scanning the room, making eye contact with pupils, standing in close proximity to a pupil, circulating round the classroom, targeting your questions, giving help to a pupil who is finding the task difficult, being consistent, avoiding unfair comparisons, not making empty threats, not making an example of a pupil, avoiding reprimanding the whole class (see Activity 9.4) There are also longer-term strategies. For example, *using behaviour contracts* – the teacher and pupil agree a list of expectations and punishments if the contract is broken. *Self-monitoring* – the pupil identifies instances of inappropriate behaviour resulting in them receiving some form of punishment. When the pupil feels they are likely to react inappropriately, the responsibility is on them to remove themselves from the situation. *Modelling acceptable behaviour* – providing examples of how they should behave in different situations.

A positive lesson climate enables pupils to demonstrate positive, appropriate behaviour. To achieve such a climate you must plan and evaluate all aspects of your teaching so that you can establish positive relationships with your pupils (see Activity 9.5).

SUMMARY

Although each teacher has their own personal approach to lesson organisation and management, they have to take account of, and fit in with, school policies and practices, e.g. on managing behaviour in the classroom. These vary between schools. It is therefore important that you develop your own organisation and management strategies, but are able to modify them according to expectations of the schools in which you teach.

Good organisation and management do not in themselves promote pupil learning. They create the time for this to occur, but more importantly enable the development of a positive lesson climate; the major factor in establishing an effective learning environment. This, in turn, supports a 'behaviour for learning' approach to pupil behaviour. The effectiveness of this approach is maximised by developing and maintaining positive relationships with your pupils. These do not happen by chance; you need to plan for them. Well organised and managed lessons allow for positive relationships to develop.

In column 1 make a list of behaviours that are inappropriate in lessons; use incidents from your own teaching and observations as well as others you can think of. In column 2 identify ways this could have been avoided. In column 3 identify action that was, or could be, taken to resolve the situation after the behaviour had occurred. Then in column 4 record the outcome of the intervention.

Type of behaviour	How it could have been prevented	Action taken after it occurred	Outcome of the intervention

Activity 9.5 Promoting a positive lesson environment

Use a piece of paper with three columns similar to the example below. For each of the actions listed, identify in column 2 how the appropriateness/effectiveness of the action could be demonstrated in a lesson. Alternatively, identify the appropriateness/effectiveness of the action in your lessons. You can do this by selecting a few actions on which to focus (in evaluating your lessons or from observation by a teacher) in any one lesson. If you complete this activity for a lesson you teach, note in column 3 what you would change next time and any development activities that would help you to be more effective.

Teacher action	How its appropriateness/effectiveness would be demonstrated OR how it was demonstrated in your lesson	What you would change next time and any development activities that would help you to be more effective
Lesson planning was appropriate		
The lesson built on the previous lesson and on pupils' prior knowledge		

Here are some suggested outcomes regarding appropriateness/effectiveness of the action in your lessons:

- Pupils knew what was going to happen in the lesson.
- Pupils were clear at the start of the lesson what they were learning, why and how it fitted with what they already knew/could do.
- The intended learning outcomes of the lesson were clearly stated at the start.
- Pupils knew at the end of the lesson whether or not they had achieved the intended learning outcomes.
- Expectations of pupils' achievement was high.
- The teacher had the knowledge to be able to move beyond telling pupils 'how to' do something to helping them to understand 'why'.
- Pupils were actively engaged in, and made sense of, their learning rather than just 'did it'.
- Pupils were helped to develop their own learning skills.
- At the start of the lesson and before each new activity pupils were clear what behaviours were needed for the learning to be successful.
- The learning needs of all pupils were understood and met.
- Assessment for learning was used effectively to help pupils reflect on what they knew/could do, reinforce the learning and set targets.
- There were high expectations of what pupils could achieve.
- Communication between teacher and pupils was good.
- The lesson had a purposeful atmosphere.
- The lesson was lively and well paced.
- The lesson activities were stimulating.

Activity 9.5 *continued*

- The organisation and management enabled pupils to spend maximum time on learning activities.
- Lesson transitions were efficient and effective.
- Rules were applied firmly and consistently.
- There were established routines.
- Positive reinforcement was used.
- Appropriate feedback and positive correction were used.
- Pupils were listened to and their answers and opinions respected.
- Expectations of pupils' behaviour was high.
- Inappropriate behaviour was pre-empted.

FURTHER READING

Ayres, H. and Gray, F. (1998) *Classroom Management: A Practical Approach for Primary and Secondary Teachers*, London: David Fulton Publishers. This book provides an easy-to-read series of activities designed to develop your management skills. It provides an overview of aspects of classroom practice combining theory with practical application. It also includes a concise chapter focusing on pupils with special education needs.

Bryson, J. (1998) *Effective Classroom Management*, London: Hodder and Stoughton. This book provides a range of checklists for classroom management, as well as wider aspects of teaching in schools, e.g. working with parents and organisation of trips and visits.

Garner, P. (2005) Behaviour for learning: a positive approach to managing classroom behaviour, in S. Capel, M. Leask and T. Turner (eds) *Learning to Teach in the Secondary School: A Companion to School Experience*, 4th edn, London: RoutledgeFalmer, pp. 136–50. This chapter provides a very useful overview of the 'behaviour for learning' approach to managing pupils' behaviour.

Chapter 10 Safe practice, risk assessment and risk management

ANNE CHAPPELL

INTRODUCTION

> Good practice is safe practice.
> (Severs *et al.*, 2003: 7)

In a culture of accountability and liability, teachers, along with other professionals, are increasingly at risk of facing litigation when things go wrong (Raymond, 1999). The fact that all physical activity contains inherent risks, and that physical education has unique risks in relation to other subjects in the National Curriculum, demands that you have specialist knowledge and understanding to ensure that all practice is safe. It is essential that you stay up to date in light of the regularity with which issues and advice relating to safety and safe practice evolve and develop.

As a teacher of physical education you have a legal, professional and moral responsibility to 'teach safety and safely' (Katene and Edmondson, 2004: 120). Once you qualify as a teacher, you have responsibility for the safety and well-being of your pupils, in both the formal learning environment of the lesson, and as part of your extra-curricular commitment. Until then, the class teachers with whom you work retain the duty of care for the pupils, allowing you to develop your knowledge, understanding and implementation of safe practice in a supported environment with a qualified teacher present. It is also important that you teach safety to pupils. Thus, this should be integral to your planning of all lessons.

Issues relating to safety in physical education are numerous and complex, and although most rely on the application of common sense (Whitlam, 2003), it is vital that you make sure that you have a good understanding of the requirements.

By the end of this chapter you should be able to:

- understand the law and documentation about safe practice;
- implement safe practice in the learning environment;
- undertake risk assessment and risk management;
- know where to go for support to ensure safe practice.

The activities in this chapter are written in such a way that you can revisit them at various points in your career, particularly as the context for your work as a physical educator changes and when you move schools.

As you undertake the activities in this chapter you need to read relevant sources listed in the further reading.

THE LAW AND DOCUMENTATION FOR SAFE PRACTICE

The School Teachers' Pay and Conditions Act (1991) sets out the legal requirements of teachers; it is vital that you understand these and how they impact on your work in the delivery of physical education. There are several key legal terms which you must know (see Activity 10.1).

Activity 10.1 Legal terms

Research the definitions of the following terms.

Term	Definition
In loco parentis	
Duty of care	
Negligence	
Liability	
Vicarious liability	

There is an increasing amount of documentation on safety that impacts on teachers' work. The Department for Education and Skills (DfES), Local Education Authorities (LEAs), schools and departments have a responsibility to produce, and regularly update, policies outlining expectations for safe practice and risk assessment which take account of current legal requirements. These policies include information for on-site and off-site activities, and provide clear guidance to support you in your practice. There are also other documents which comprehensively address issues relating to safety across the school and specifically in physical education (see, for example, BAALPE, 2004; Croner, 2004).

In order for the policies to have any value, and for you to ensure that you fully understand your responsibilities, as well as protecting yourself against accusations of negligence and claims for liability, it is essential that you familiarise yourself with them (see Activity 10.2).

SAFE PRACTICE IN THE LEARNING ENVIRONMENT

The National Curriculum for Physical Education (NCPE) (DfEE/QCA, 1999: 39) legally requires that:

> pupils should be taught . . . to recognise hazards, assess consequent risks and take steps to control the risks to themselves and others; to use information to assess the immediate and cumulative risks; to manage their environment to ensure the health and safety of themselves and others; to explain the steps they take to control risks.

A teacher requires sound knowledge and understanding of the key principles for safe exercise that apply across physical education (BAALPE, 2004; Norris, 1999) in order to support the development of a safe learning environment. Observing teachers provides a wealth of valuable information about safe practice in lessons, how it is planned (you might also want to look at schemes of work, units of work and lesson plans) and how it is established (see Activities 10.3 and 10.4).

It is very important that pupils are involved in supporting a safe learning environment via expectations, procedures and routines and that they have ownership of knowledge and understanding about safety: their full involvement is significant in ensuring safe practice. Having looked at the teacher's role in developing the environment for learning, it is then important for you to begin your own planning by finding out what the pupils you will be teaching already know (see Activity 10.5).

Based on the information collected in the first five activities you can begin to list 'ground rules' that you will negotiate with pupils, and begin to reflect on the ways that you might include these within a scheme of work, units of work and lesson plans (see Activity 10.6).

As well as understanding the organisational implications for safety, you also need current knowledge and understanding of safe exercise, including contra-indications in physical activity based on current scientific research. Pupils also need to understand safe exercise; indeed, they must be taught the 'knowledge and understanding of fitness and health' as part of the NCPE 'Programme of Study' (DfEE/QCA, 1999: 6). For example, in teaching pupils about preparation of the body for physical activity, it is important that you clearly explain the elements of a warm-up and the correct way to stretch, much of which you can also apply to the process of preparing the body for rest or cooling down (see Activity 10.7).

Pupils need to know and understand why there are some activities that have more risks than benefits and so as the teacher you must be clear about these (BAALPE, 2004; Donovan et al., 1988) (see Activity 10.8).

It is also essential that you are fully aware of how to manage the potentially dangerous issues which arise on a lesson by lesson basis (BAALPE, 2004). These issues can be procedural (e.g. what pupils are wearing) or based on lesson content. Some of these issues relate to the cultural background of pupils that you work with and so it is key for you to handle them with understanding and sensitivity (see Activity 10.9).

Activity 10.2 Finding documentation

Locate the following documents in your school and identify the key information that each contains, as the example demonstrates.

Document	Location	Key information
The Head's Legal Guide (Croner, 2004)	Head teacher's office .	*Detailed guidelines on all legal aspects of the school including teacher's pay and conditions, and health and safety*
Safe Practice in Physical Education and School Sport (BAALPE, 2004)		
LEA Guidelines for Physical Education and School Sport		
LEA Guidelines for Educational Visits		
School Health and Safety Policy		
First Aid Policy and Accident Record		
Department Health and Safety Policy		
Department Risk Assessment Record		
Any others		

Activity 10.3 Procedures and routines in physical education

Observe a complete physical education lesson – starting as pupils arrive at the changing room. Make a note of all the procedures and routines (adding any that are not included here), and identify the safety implications for each.

Routine	Observation	Safety implications
Have pupils removed all jewellery? How is this managed?		
Have any medical conditions been taken into account? What about the wearing of glasses? How are 'excuse' notes handled?		
Is pupils' clothing appropriate and do they have appropriate footwear? How is this managed? How is the wearing of headscarves managed?		
What instructions does the teacher give the pupils prior to leaving the changing room?		
What is the routine for taking equipment to the working area?		
How is equipment such as cones laid out?		
How does the teacher distribute bats, balls, sticks, etc.?		
How does the teacher gain the attention of the class in the teaching area?		
What strategy does the teacher use to place the pupils into groups?		
How does the teacher organise teams for games?		
What routines are used for the start and finish of an activity, e.g. are the children called in?		
What routines are used for the removal and dismantling of large apparatus during the lesson, e.g. gymnastics?		
Others		

Activity 10.4 Providing a safe environment

Identify an area of activity which you need to target for development in relation to understanding appropriate safety issues. Observe a lesson and respond to the following in order to develop a better awareness of the type of factors teachers need to take into account when planning for a safe environment.

In what ways could the lesson be hazardous?

What measures has the teacher taken to minimise the safety risk?

Write a list of questions to ask the teacher on any aspect of safety within the lesson.

Write a summary of your discussions with the teacher after the lesson.

Activity 10.5 What do the pupils know about safety?

Speak to pupils and note what they know about safety using the following questions and ones that you devise based on your research into safety. You may wish to use these types of questions with pupils when you first work with them, and at the end of a unit of work to assess their learning.

1   What is safety?
2   What is risk?
3   Why is safety important?
4   What do you do to make sure you and the pupils around you are safe?
5   What would put you and the pupils around you at risk?
6   What does the teacher do to make sure that you are safe?
7   What advice would you give young children about staying safe during physical education or in sporting activities?

Activity 10.6 Setting ground rules to support safe practice

Following observations of lessons, conversations with pupils and research into safe practice, write a list of general ground rules that you will develop with the pupils that you teach and reinforce in every lesson.

1   All jewellery and adornment to be completely removed for every lesson.

2   ....
....
....

3   ....
....
....

4   ....
....
....

5   ....
....
....

6   ....
....
....

7   ....
....
....

8   ....
....
....

9   ....
....
....

10 ....
....
....

Activity 10.7 Effective preparation for exercise

Elements of a warm-up

Research and make notes about the purpose of the following elements of an effective warm-up for a physical education lesson.

Element	Purpose	Examples	Contra-indications
Mobilising activities			
Pulse-raising activities			
Stretching			

Types of stretching

Research and compare the following types of stretching taking into account the potential risk factors for pupils.

Type	Definition	Value for pupils	Contra-indications
Static stretching			
Dynamic stretching			
Ballistic stretching			

You may want to do the same for mobilising and pulse-raising activities.

Activity 10.8 Contra-indications and safe exercise

Investigate the potential dangers in the following exercises which have been identified as being contra-indicated. Find out what the safe alternatives are.

Exercise	Potential risk	Safe alternative
V-sits		
Straight leg sit-ups		
Straight leg toe touches		
Straight leg side bends		
Burpees		
Full head circles		
Hurdle stretch		
Sit and reach		
Deep knee bends		
Hyper-extension of the back (standing and lying)		
Ballistic stretching		

Activity 10.9 Safety considerations

Find out from literature and colleagues about the following factors in physical education and consider how you should manage them to ensure minimal risk.

Procedural

Removal of jewellery	
Appropriate clothing	
Appropriate footwear	
Medical conditions	
Wearing of glasses	
Wearing of headscarves	
Management of excuse notes	

Lesson content

Order of activities	*Ensure the order of activities allows the body to be appropriately prepared, e.g. mobilise shoulders before the cervical vertebrae, and lumbar vertebrae before performing lateral flexion to reduce the risk of injury*
Contra-indicated exercises	
Rest	
Progression	
Joint alignment	
Use of momentum	
High impact exercises	
Lack of stability	

There are different safety implications for different learning environments. As well as the procedures in place for safe practice in relation to physical activity, there is also the requirement of knowledge and understanding of policy and procedure relating to those activities which take place on and off site outside of timetabled lesson time (see Activity 10.10).

Activity 10.10 Extra-curricular activities

These activities may take place over a period of time as you look at each element as the opportunity arises. For the following activities identify which school staff you need support from, the guidance documentation you need and any paperwork that you need to complete.

Activity	Staff support required	Guidance document	Completed document
An on-site lunchtime club for pupils (e.g. swimming club in the school pool)	Head of department and lifeguard	*Safe Practice* (BAALPE, 2004); Department health and safety policy, including risk assessment	None

Do the same for:

- an evening competition off-site at another school (e.g. gymnastics competition or volleyball match);
- involvement in an off-site afternoon event (e.g. borough athletics meeting);
- an off-site educational trip during the day (e.g. to a theatre to watch a dance performance or a university laboratory for examination coursework);
- residential trips (e.g. an outdoor and adventurous activities week).

RISK ASSESSMENT AND MANAGEMENT

As a physical education teacher you are expected to identify foreseeable risks that may result in injury (risk assessment), and take reasonable practicable steps to reduce the risk to an acceptable level (risk management) (BAALPE, 2004). The Health and Safety Executive (HSE, 1999: 2) identify that a risk assessment is 'nothing more than a careful examination of what, in your work, could cause harm to people' and that this is done 'so that you can weigh up whether you have taken enough precautions to prevent harm'. They outline five clear steps that need to be taken in risk assessment and management:

1 Look for the hazards.
2 Decide who might be harmed, and how.
3 Evaluate the risks and decide whether precautions are adequate or more needs to be done.
4 Record your findings.
5 Review your assessment and revise it as necessary.

(ibid.: 3)

The BAALPE document *Safe Practice in Physical Education and School Sport* (2004) clearly identifies the information needed to support effective risk assessment and management. This document is increasingly used in the legal environment to guide decisions about negligence and liability. The areas which you need to consider initially are those of pupils; facilities; the six areas of activity in the NCPE; and environmental conditions which directly impact upon your work. In identifying the potential risks, problems or issues you are more informed; thus, making risk management more effective (see Activities 10.11, 10.12, 10.13 and 10.14).

Activity 10.11 Accidents

Review accidents that could have happened in the physical education setting, identifying the potential outcomes for accusations of negligence by the teacher, depending on the circumstances, and possible measures for risk control.

Incident	Issue of responsibility	Risk control
Stud earring ripped out of a pupil's ear during a netball lesson leaving a wound requiring stitches	*Teacher accountable for pupils being appropriately dressed for the activity (BAALPE guidelines)*	*All jewellery to be removed in the changing rooms at the start of the lesson*
Discus fatally hitting a pupil on the back of the head		
Pupil broke a wrist having run into a wall in the sports hall using hands to break the run during a wet weather activity		
Pupil sustained severe concussion and a cut requiring stitches when a trampoline fell while the pupil was assisting the teacher in wheeling it to the side of the gym		

Activity 10.12 Facilities and risk assessment

Using the example, for each of the other facilities used for physical education (plus any others you can identify), note any potential hazards for which you need to plan and the measures you could take to manage and reduce the risk. Do the risks vary depending upon the activity taking place in the facility? You can also use the school and departmental risk assessment documents to help you.

Facility	Potential hazard	Activity	Risk management
Gymnasium	*Trampolines round the edges of the room*	*Pose a significant hazard for games activities*	*Mark/cone off the area and ensure that pupils are fully aware of the area which is off limits*
Sports hall			
Dance studio			
Hard courts			
Field			
Swimming pool			
Others			

Identify the important safety considerations unique to each of the six areas of activity in the NCPE (DfEE/QCA, 1999).

Area of activity	Unique safety issues
Athletic activities	
Dance activities	
Games activities	
Gymnastic activities	
Outdoor and adventurous activities	
Swimming activities	

Activity 10.14 Environmental considerations

List your responsibilities to pupils in various weather conditions. Check the department and school policies to see what guidance has been given on risk management for each.

Weather condition	Potential problems	Solution
Sunshine (hot)	*Sun burn* *Dehydration* *Concentration difficulties* *Fatigue*	*Pupils to bring sunscreen and water to all lessons* *Shade areas to be used at appropriate intervals in the lesson* *High intensity activity to be avoided* *Pupils to wear lightweight, light-coloured clothing* *Indoor facilities to be used if necessary*
Rain		
Thunder and lightning		
Hail		
Wind		
Low temperatures		
Frost		
Snow		

SUPPORT TO ENSURE SAFE PRACTICE

You are expected to have the necessary knowledge and skills to undertake your work safely and it is your responsibility to seek advice and support if you are in doubt about any aspect of your work (Severs *et al.*, 2003). It is important that you have an understanding of the key requirements for your professional responsibilities to facilitate a better understanding of your learning needs. It is essential that you discuss particular areas of identified need with your mentor and focus on them as part of your learning. Having referred to 'safe practice in physical education' (BAALPE, 2004: 2), list the professional responsibilities and key requirements of you as a teacher, in order to reflect upon all the vital factors to ensure that your practice throughout physical education is safe (see Activity 10.15).

It is important to recognise that seeking support is both professional and prudent. There are many sources of support available. It is good practice to discuss issues with colleagues in your department, as well as other colleagues in the school. If you need to seek wider support, then you can contact the following: your union; your professional association (e.g. Physical Education Association of the United Kingdom; PEAUK or BAALPE); or the LEA.

CONCLUSION

An NQT recently stated during her first term in school following a particularly unpleasant accident, 'it is horrible to learn the hard way'. The most distressing thing for her was that, in hindsight, she recognised that the circumstances prior to the accident could have been managed in a more appropriate way. Fortunately, no legal action was taken but, had it been, the teacher would have been put in a very difficult situation and the potential outcome could have been detrimental to her career. This illustrates that:

> In the event of an accident to a pupil, the teacher should be in a position to demonstrate, if necessary to a court, that all the relevant safety precautions have been taken in order to answer any allegations of negligence or breach of a duty of care.
>
> (Croner, 2003, CD-ROM)

One way would be to undertake a detailed audit of health and safety practice in the department in which you are working and familiarise yourself with every aspect of your professional environment. This information will support your planning for safety (see Activity 10.16).

Another way you can do this is to consider examples of things that have gone wrong in physical education and the detailed legal analysis and final outcome (e.g. Katene and Edmondson, 2004; PEAUK, 2000 onwards; Raymond, 1999; Whitlam, 2004). These case studies provide a valuable stimulus for critical thought and reflection about your knowledge and practice. They are also a useful tool for discussion.

Finally, BAALPE (2004: 13) identifies elements of good practice that minimise the risks of harm to the pupils and negligence on your part. These provide you with a guide to enable you to reflect on what you do in a proactive, effective, professional manner:

- appropriate and up-to-date qualifications for staff;
- appropriate steps taken to guarantee safety;
- pupils are fully aware;
- pupils are fully prepared;
- visits are organised using clear procedures supported by policy;
- records are kept (registers, lesson plans);
- teachers are kept up to date on Health and Safety;
- regular risk assessments are undertaken and recorded;
- activities are undertaken in line with 'good regular and approved practice'.

Activity 10.15 Appropriate challenge versus acceptable risk

Identify the professional responsibilities inherent in physical education and school sport, highlighting the key requirements for each.

	Professional responsibility	Key requirements
People	Teachers	
	Pupils	
Context	Procedures	
	Physical education equipment	
	Physical education facilities	
Organisation	Preparation	
	Teaching style and class organisation	

Activity 10.16 Health and safety audit

Complete the audit in Raymond (1999: 157–60), seeking advice where necessary.

SUMMARY

As you can see from this chapter there is a lot to consider in teaching 'safety and safely' (Katene and Edmondson, 2004: 120). It would be unrealistic to expect you to know everything about every element of safe practice and risk assessment in physical education when you start in your first teaching post. It is, however, imperative that you keep the development of knowledge and understanding at the top of your professional agenda and practice from the outset of your ITE. It is also important that you know where to get advice and seek advice and support whenever you feel it is needed.

FURTHER READING

Within the list of further readings are texts which have been specifically identified to support you in completing the activities included in this chapter. Those which do not relate to specific activities will provide background reading to support your understanding of this complex area.

BAALPE (2004) *Safe Practice in Physical Education and School Sport*, Leeds: Coachwise Solutions.
Activities 10.1–10.16.

Croner (2004) *The Head's Legal Guide*, Kingston-upon-Thames: WoltersKluwer
Activity 10.2.

DfEE/QCA (Department for Education and Employment/Qualifications and Curriculum Authority) (1999) *Physical Education: The National Curriculum for England*, London: QCA.
Activities 10.5 and 10.13.

Donovan, G., McNamara, J. and Gianoli, P. (1988) *Exercise Danger*, Floreat Park: Wellness Australia.
Activities 10.7 and 10.8.

Harris, J. and Elbourn, J. (2002) *Warming Up and Cooling Down*, Leeds: Human Kinetics.
Activities 10.7 and 10.8.

Health and Safety Executive (1999) *Five Steps to Risk Assessment*, Sudbury: Health and Safety Executive.
Hopper, B., Grey, J. and Maude, P. (2003) *Teaching Physical Education in the Primary School*, London: RoutledgeFalmer.
Activities 10.6 and 10.13.

Katene, W. and Edmondson, G. (2004) Teaching safely and safety in PE, in S. Capel (ed.) *Learning to Teach Physical Education in the Secondary School*, London: RoutledgeFalmer.
Activity 10.1.

Norris, C.M. (1999) *The Complete Guide to Stretching*, London: A & C Black.
Activities 10.7 and 10.8.

PEAUK (2000–present) Physical education and the law, *British Journal of Teaching Physical Education*, Vol. 31 onwards.
Activities 10.10–10.13.

Raymond, C. (ed.) (1999) *Safety Across the Curriculum*, London: RoutledgeFalmer.
Activities 10.1 and 10.15.

Severs, J., Whitlam, P. and Woodhouse, J. (2003) *Safety and Risk in Primary School Physical Education: A Guide for Teachers*, London: Routledge.
Activities 10.1, 10.9, 10.13 and 10.15.

Whitlam, P. (2003) Risk management principles, in J. Severs, P. Whitlam and J. Woodhouse (eds) (2003) *Safety and Risk in Primary School Physical Education: A Guide for Teachers*, London: Routledge.
Activities 10.1, 10.3 and 10.4.

Whitlam, P. (2004) *Case Law in Physical Education and School Sport*, Leeds: Coachwise Solutions.
Activities 10.3, 10.4, 10.10–10.14.

Chapter 11 Maximising the achievement of all pupils

JEAN O'NEILL AND KAREN PACK

INTRODUCTION

In your work in school it should be obvious that pupils have specific individual needs in addition to needs common to all pupils of that age. These needs may relate to, for example, their ability/disability, gender, race, religion or cultural background. The diversity of individual needs is challenging because *each* pupil has the right to an education which enables him/her to fulfil their potential. In providing equality of opportunity for all pupils, you have to be able to plan for inclusion through differentiated teaching and learning, then regularly review and evaluate how effective you were.

By the end of this chapter you should be able to:

- understand 'equality of opportunity' and 'inclusion' for teaching and learning;
- understand teaching from a learning perspective;
- understand the importance of 'differentiation' in teaching and learning;
- identify some possible teaching strategies to support pupils' specific individual needs;
- challenge gifted and talented pupils within and outside of physical education lessons.

In order to maximise every pupil's achievement you must take account of these 'differences'. In doing so you may make an obvious response, such as giving specific help/advice. However, pupil differences do not always require a response from the teacher (see Activities 11.1 and 11.2).

Activity 11.2 illustrates the close relationship between teaching and learning. Although the teacher sets a task, he or she must observe and take into account the pupils' responses in order to set the subsequent task; otherwise teaching would become a prescribed set of instructions to pupils which disregard their individual needs.

Activity 11.1   Identifying differences in a class

Observe a physical education class which you have not observed or taught before. Do not talk to the teacher about the class beforehand. As you observe the lesson write down in column 1 of the worksheet given in Activity 11.2 any pupil 'differences' you see and hear. Talk to the teacher after the lesson and see how well your record of 'differences' matches what the teacher perceives.

Activity 11.2 Do the 'differences' impact on the teaching and learning?

Observe the same class as for Activity 11.1 and note the impact of the difference on teaching and learning and how the teacher caters for the difference. Then record what you would do to cater for pupils' individual needs if you taught this class.

Pupil difference	What is its impact on teaching and learning?	How does the teacher cater for this difference?	What would you do to cater for this need?
e.g. Pupil who is partially deaf	Pupil calls out loudly if unsure what to do. Other pupils stand and stop working	Places him with a hearing 'partner'	

EQUALITY OF OPPORTUNITY

Paying due regard to the statutory entitlement for all pupils means providing 'equality of opportunity' for every pupil. This does not mean treating them all in the same way but ensures that you know and understand the needs of each pupil and act upon these in order to maximise his/her learning. However,

> [I]t would be a mistake to equate *access* with *opportunity* and it is important to appreciate the distinction between the two. In some schools pupils may be said to have the same *access* to curriculum physical education, regardless of, for example, their ability, sex, religion or ethnic background. But it may not be the case that these children have equal *opportunities* . . . in different activities.
>
> (DES, 1991: 15)

This is not the place to examine the relationship between these two concepts, nor to examine 'access' issues in depth. However, it is important for you to recognise that in physical education the structure and delivery of the curriculum are (still) frequently based on gender (cultural) expectations and assumptions, e.g. girls are required to play netball and boys play football simply because they are different sexes and the activities are perceived to be appropriate 'feminine' and 'masculine' activities. This is not the case in every school but in our experience it is very prevalent, with the result that many pupils are denied equality of access.

There are four principles which underpin equality of opportunity: entitlement (pupils' right to access the physical education curriculum); accessibility (all physical education lessons are barrier-free and meet the diverse needs in the class); integration (recognises the benefit of inclusive education and the positive outcomes that can be achieved for all pupils); and integrity (teaching and learning values the adaptations and modifications made in order to plan effectively for the inclusion of all pupils) (see Vickerman, 2004: 157–9). Vickerman (ibid.: 154) also explains that all pupils have 'a fundamental right to an inclusive education, which is supported in England through legislation'. The National Curriculum Statutory Inclusion Statement (DfEE/QCA, 1999) explains this in more detail and we suggest that you read that statement (see Activities 11.3 and 11.4).

INCLUSION

Although you may be familiar with the National Curriculum for Physical Education (NCPE) you may not realise that the concept of a 'national curriculum' is an integral part of the Education Reform Act (1988) and as such is founded on a set of principles which include 'entitlement for all' pupils. In this entitlement inclusion is a central theme. The statutory inclusion statement in the National Curriculum sets out three principles that are essential to developing a more inclusive curriculum:

1   Setting suitable learning challenges.
2   Responding to pupils' diverse learning needs.
3   Overcoming potential barriers to learning and assessment for individuals and groups of pupils.

These provide the basis for providing effective learning opportunities for all pupils (DfEE/QCA, 1999: 28) in which the teacher modifies, as necessary, the programmes of study to include all pupils and provide them with relevant and appropriately challenging work at each Key Stage (see Activity 11.5). Now *build upon* your understanding of the application of 'inclusion' (see Activity 11.6).

However, there may be occasions where a pupil would have more chance of succeeding if s/he were *segregated* in some way. For example, it is not possible to fully include a physically disabled child in a contact game such as rugby. However, they could participate in a less strenuous invasion game nearby or could be encouraged to referee or coach. Thus, partial inclusion enables the pupil to maintain some involvement with the class in a way which maximises his/her learning opportunities.

Activity 11.3 How accessible is the physical education curriculum?

Obtain a copy of the physical education curriculum in a mixed secondary school and answer the following questions (you may also have to talk to the teacher):

1 Are all the physical education activities taught to all of the pupils? If not, which activities are taught in mixed sex groups and which in single sex groups? Why is this so? Do you agree with the reason(s) given? Why/why not?
2 Are all the physical education activities experienced by pupils in mixed classes? If they are not, why is this so? Do you agree with the reason(s) given?
3 Does the provision of physical education activities vary according to the age of the pupils? Why? Do you agree with the reason(s) given? Why/why not?

Activity 11.4 School policies on equality of opportunity

Read your school's whole-school and physical education policies on the provision of equality of opportunity. Do this activity in relation to both the whole school and the physical education policies.

Do each of the policies reflect a commitment to working within the four principles of equality of opportunity?

What are your reasons for this?

Which of the four principles, in your view, are strong aspects of this policy?

Why?

Discuss any aspects of both policies which you are less certain about.

What conclusion(s) have you reached as a result of the discussion?

How will these conclusions affect your teaching of physical education?

Re-read the section on inclusion in the NCPE (DfEE/QCA, 1999: 28–36) then refer back to Activity 11.2 and identify which of these principles were addressed by the teacher in each of the examples you recorded.

Activity 11.6 Observing inclusive teaching

Decide on a class with a diversity of pupils within it. Select and observe the same pupils throughout the lesson. With the teacher's help during the lesson note whether any of the following occurred:

1   Pupils were given adapted, modified or alternative tasks and/or equipment which were similar to that which the rest of the class experienced.
2   Record the *specific support* from at least one other person without which they could not participate in all the tasks. If this did not occur, leave blank but be aware of the reason(s) for the lack of specific support.

Physical education activity: _____ Year: _____

Which pupil?	Description of task adaptation	Reason(s) for the task	Who supported him/her?	Reason for the support?
John – gifted pupil	Served from the baseline	To challenge him		
Joanne – partially sighted	Used a slow-bouncing ball and large-headed racquet	To give her a better chance of hitting the ball		
Paul – autistic			Learning Support Assistant (LSA)	He was very reluctant to speak to any other pupils

To what extent were each of the pupils you observed taught so that their learning was maximised? Which of the three teaching principles on inclusion (DfEE/QCA, 1999: 28) were used? Give reasons for your comments.

START WITH THE *LEARNERS'* NEEDS WHEN PLANNING LESSONS

Clearly, all teachers are challenged every day to help each pupil to achieve their potential. To do this, you should view your teaching from a *learning* perspective. Rather than look at instructional strategies, you focus on pupils' *learning* and what you need to do to improve/maximise their learning. After all, your aim as a teacher is to empower pupils by shifting the responsibility for learning from yourself to them. Physical education teachers – particularly when teaching skills, frequently give a 'demonstration' of good movement, which the pupils watch and then strive to replicate. Less prevalent is the use of 'indirect teaching', where some of the demonstrations of good movement, decision-making and feedback tasks are *shifted to the pupils*. Here the teacher must communicate to the pupils exactly what their responsibility is in the learning process and make sure that they understand what they are supposed to be doing before they are sent off to do it (see Rink, 1999). It *shares* the teaching and learning with the pupils, but in order for it to be *inclusive* all pupils must be able to succeed at the task. Indeed,

> The task provided to the learner must be individually appropriate; the learner must have a clear idea of what he or she is expected to do and be motivated to engage at a high level with the task; the learner must have sufficient opportunity to learn the task and the learner must receive information on their performance.
>
> (ibid.: 149)

The 'spectrum of teaching styles' (Mosston and Ashworth, 2002) sets out how this sharing of responsibility for pupils' learning and inclusion could occur. For example, in the reciprocal style *pupils* provide feedback to other pupils and the teacher's role is to communicate with the 'teachers', not directly with the 'performers'. This could be differentiated further by, for example, some (e.g. the more able) pupils learning reciprocally whilst the teacher works *during the same task* with other (less able) pupils in the practice style. Read about Mosston's teaching styles and be aware of how and to what extent pupils are given responsibility for their learning and how the use of more than one style can maximise the learning of a task for *all* pupils. However, teachers need preparation before using the various teaching styles; if you use it in your lessons without preparation, your teaching is unlikely to be successful (see Activity 11.7).

Once you have a good understanding of your pupils' needs and abilities you learn how to teach more effectively by including the principle of 'differentiation'.

DIFFERENTIATED TEACHING AND LEARNING

'Differentiation' is not a single event; rather, it is a continuous process. It involves knowing your pupils' needs, planning to meet them in a way that enables each pupil to progress their learning and achieve their full potential and, after the lesson, evaluating the appropriateness of the learning outcomes. This is explained further in Vickerman (2004: 153–64) and Capel *et al.* (1999: 134). It also means that you need to understand the content you are teaching. Differentiation can be achieved in a number of ways including differentiation by:

- *Outcome* – the same task is set for the whole class which is open enough for all pupils to do it successfully. This 'involves recognising the variety of needs in a class, planning to meet those needs, providing appropriate delivery and evaluation of the effectiveness of the activities in order to maximise the achievement of individual pupils (NCET, 1993: 21).
- *Task* – pupils are given different, but related tasks according to their ability level (see Activity 11.8).

On the lesson plan for the best lesson you have taught recently, write 'a' next to tasks that used instructional/directed teaching and 'b' next to tasks where the pupils were more responsible for their own learning. Add them up and write the totals here:

a = ... b = ... Did you do more of a or b? Why? Write your reasons here:

If you taught mainly in an instructional style, how could you change some of the tasks to include the pupils in their learning? Look again at your lesson plan and write your comments here:

It may help you to answer this question by observing a physical education teacher who encourages pupils to be responsible for some of their learning, by including tasks which require *the pupils* to give feedback and to make decisions.

Think about your teaching generally and answer these questions:

1   Do you think that you rely mainly on giving instructions, demonstrations and feedback to the class in your lessons?

2   To what extent do you teach in a more indirect way so that pupils have to think more for themselves? How do you include all pupils in this?

3   How can you change your teaching to include more indirect teaching?

4   Do the answers to these two questions vary according to which physical education activity you are teaching? Why? Should they?

Remember that ALL physical education activities should be delivered in an inclusive way, otherwise how can the pupils' various needs be met?

Activity 11.8   What teaching strategies would you use to include these pupils?

For each case study below, suggest a possible teaching strategy to solve, or at least alleviate the problem. Some possible responses are given on the website.

1   Joanna, Year 7, has a sight defect and is frightened by the lines on the pool bottom

Behaviour: reluctant to swim, prefers standing in the shallow end, disruptive to nearby swimmers.

Possible teaching strategies: . . . .
. . . .
. . . .

Why have you included those strategies? . . . .
. . . .
. . . .

2   A mixed school with a strong house system has a big decrease in participation for the inter-house swimming galas at Key Stage 4

Behaviour: non-participants calling out/whistling to swimmers – particularly to the girls; few girls swimming.

Possible teaching strategies . . . .
. . . .
. . . .

Why have you included those strategies? . . . .
. . . .
. . . .

3   Emma, a gifted athlete, is very well developed for her age in both height and physical maturity but is reluctant to participate in physical education

Behaviour: frequently forgets her kit, 'hangs around' the physical education department, appears miserable but is interested in physical education.

Reason for her behaviour: very self-conscious about her physical maturity and giftedness.

Possible teaching strategies . . . .
. . . .
. . . .

Why have you included those strategies? . . . .
. . . .
. . . .

continued . . .

4   John is a good swimmer but he became overweight and now opts out of swimming

Behaviour: frequently forgets his kit, brings excusal notes from home.

Reason for his behaviour: too embarrassed to wear swimming trunks.

Possible teaching strategies . . . .
. . . .

Why have you included those strategies? . . . .
. . . .

5   Several Afro-Caribbean boys are under-achieving in athletics lessons

Behaviour: excessive noise and 'larking about', ridiculing pupils who are doing well, lack concentration.

Reason for their behaviour: they think that other pupils and the physical education teacher expect them to live up to a racial stereotype – that they will excel in athletics. So to prevent 'failure' they decide not to risk 'doing their best'.

Possible teaching strategies . . . .
. . . .

Why have you included those strategies? . . . .
. . . .

6   Stefan, a Romanian asylum-seeker with his family, although talented and very enthusiastic in physical education, is always slow to react to instructions and tasks

Behaviour: unsociable, wary of advice or assistance.

Reason for his behaviour: English is an additional language for him and he fails to understand much of what is being said quickly enough to show his full potential. It annoys him!

Possible teaching strategies . . . .
. . . .

Why have you included those strategies? . . . .
. . . .

Think of other examples you have experienced. What factors alerted you to the issue? How was it resolved? Refer back to Activity 11.1 and suggest whether the teacher could have used other strategies for each example given.

While you are learning to teach it is easier for you to think of the class as consisting of (say, three) different ability bands rather than trying to set tasks for every individual. Even the best teachers would find that difficult! Therefore, in planning lessons include differentiated learning outcomes which challenge each ability band (see also Chapter 12). After several lessons *individual pupils' needs within* each ability band become more apparent and require more specific differentiated tasks. For example, the top ability band might include a talented pupil who is clearly much more able than anyone else in that activity. This pupil would start with the same differentiated task as others in the group, but would quickly need to be given another related task which is more difficult; in order to maximise his/her learning.

SOME POSSIBLE TEACHING STRATEGIES TO INCLUDE PUPILS WITH SPECIFIC INDIVIDUAL NEEDS

If the lesson is not differentiated, some exceptionally able and enthusiastic pupils may feel under-challenged, while other pupils who do not willingly take part in physical education are not motivated. A variety of factors such as pupils' physical disability, body build/type, gender, religion, race, cultural background and grasp of English, for example may contribute to their response. Even the physical education kit, changing and showering procedures can be problematic. Some factors to consider are given below. You should complete the relevant case study in Activity 11.8 at the end of each example.

The physical education activities

While you cannot or should not base your curriculum on likes and dislikes of pupils, be aware that activities such as swimming, gymnastics, rugby and dance may be threatening to some pupils. The *fear* factor is a major reason why some pupils 'opt out' by 'forgetting' their kit. You can use various strategies to ease these pupils into the activity and gradually increase their confidence. In swimming, for example, group similar abilities together. It may be better to have single-sex lessons for older pupils – why? Do not start with stroke technique – why? Maybe you can have a health focus in your lessons, asking reluctant pupils to lead aspects of the lesson. Perhaps start them off with a dry side lesson and gradually as their interest and confidence develop they may become more willing to participate. You should differentiate by task or by outcome (see Activity 11.9).

Sex groupings

Mixed sex lessons have both advantages and disadvantages. Some pupils, e.g. girls at Key Stage 4, may choose *inactivity* in a mixed-sex lesson. Consider whether single-sexed groups for some activities would result in greater participation. In mixed-sex groups let the pupils choose their own peers to work with and consider the equipment being used. Would adapted rules create greater equality of opportunity?

Physical maturity and body shape

At Key Stage 3 there will be a few pupils who have had an early growth spurt. Consequently, they may feel clumsy and awkward in lessons. This can show itself in various ways, such as forgetting kit, withdrawn behaviour or loudness and other means of attention seeking. Physical differences within a class may make contact sports difficult for some boys. Also, for example, a large pupil with few body management skills may find their maturity or body shape embarrassing and feel threatened when required to work in mixed-sex groups or when supporting each other in gymnastics. This will often be a cause of non-participation; avoid drawing further attention to these pupils.

Activity 11.9 Differentiating by task and by outcome

Below are some tasks differentiated by task and by outcome. Add one example for swimming, OAA and dance and then for some of the lessons you are going to teach.

Differentiation by outcome

- (Gymnastics) 'On the apparatus travel in different ways, varying the height at which you work.'
- (Rugby) 'Pass the ball backwards to your partner as you move from this marker to the next. Pass the ball to each other 3, 5, 7 times.'
- (Athletics) 'Practise your fastest sprint start.'

Swimming . . . .
. . . .
. . . .
OAA . . . .
. . . .
. . . .
Dance . . . .
. . . .
. . . .

Differentiation by task – following on from the tasks above:

- (Gymnastics) 'As you travel, keep most of your body away from the apparatus and include low, middle and high levels' (most able); 'As you travel, grip the apparatus with your body and move from the low to middle level' (least able).
- (Rugby) 'Make sure that you are both running fast before the ball is passed' (most able); 'Start jogging then pass the ball to your partner' (least able).
- (Athletics) 'Use the crouch start' (most able); 'Make sure that you have one foot in front of the other and are leaning forwards before starting' (least able).

Swimming . . . .
. . . .
. . . .
OAA . . . .
. . . .
. . . .
Dance . . . .
. . . .
. . . .

Clothing

The appropriateness of physical education clothing can be a major factor in encouraging participation. Probably the most contentious is swimwear for older pupils. In gymnastics or dance, leotards are an item of clothing which many girls find embarrassing. Is it more appropriate to have both sexes wearing shorts and T-shirts for many physical activities?

Changing facilities

Think back to your early experiences of physical education and it is highly likely that the enforced taking of showers will be high on your list of unpleasant memories – and you *liked* physical education! If the facilities have communal showers with cold water (and if they are dirty or need redecorating), could you justify the appropriateness of making pupils take a shower? You can encourage cleanliness by asking all pupils to wash in the basins if necessary.

CHALLENGING THE GIFTED AND TALENTED PUPILS IN PHYSICAL EDUCATION

Pupils who are exceptionally able and exhibit higher levels of attainment than their peers in the same age group, frequently achieving aspects of the 'exceptional performance' level in the attainment target (DfEE/QCA, 1999) are gifted and talented. These pupils usually make up the top 5–10 per cent of each year group in a school (DfES, 2001a). In physical education 'gifted and talented' has been further defined by using these performance indicators:

Level 1 = County representation.
Level 2 = Regional representation.
Level 3 = National representation.

These pupils should be challenged through differentiated tasks and outcomes. Additionally, teachers need to cater for their needs outside curriculum time. A structured mentoring programme will enable each pupil to pursue extension and enrichment tasks.

In the Physical Education, School Sport and Club Links (PESSCL) strategy (DfES/DCMS, 2003), there is a 'gifted and talented' strand which seeks to improve participation in sporting and dance opportunities by the most physically able young people. This document also encapsulates the importance of effective partnership working with other physical education departments and with community-based sport and dance agencies to create a talent register for their locality and ensure that resources are used *to maximise each pupil's learning* (see also Chapter 13 and access these websites for more information: www.nc.uk.net/gt/pe/index.htm; www.talentladder.org.uk) (see Activities 11.10 and 11.11).

Possible strategies for teaching talented performers

1   Ask them to lead aspects of the warm-up/cool-down (they will have experienced very detailed warm-ups relevant to their sports). When working on fitness elements, set them tougher challenges and ask them to focus on areas of fitness identified by their coaches.
2   Set smaller, more difficult targets, i.e. in tennis when teaching serving, lay out hoops, or use cans to challenge them to be more accurate. Communicate with their coaches. What are they currently working on to improve and can you fit this into your lesson planning? In football/hockey, allow them one touch before passing. Bring Speed, Agility, Quickness (SAQ) into your skills development. This can be made very specific to individual needs.
3   Using their experiences of tactics and strategies, ask them to plan, e.g. systems of defence and attack in games. Integrate this into your lesson planning.

Activity 11.10 Identifying gifted and talented pupils

Using these questions as a starting point, audit the provision for gifted and talented pupils in your school:

- What methods of identification are used to identify gifted and talented pupils?
- How far are parents engaged in this identification and in providing support?
- What emphasis is given to developing the skills of independent learning?
- What are the implications for staffing and staff development?
- How effective are the systems for monitoring the impact of programmes in terms of outcomes for pupils?
- To what extent do the subject-specific approaches build on additional programmes by focusing on what constitutes challenging expectations and good practice?
- What is the mechanism for linking gifted and talented pupils with outside clubs, etc.?

Activity 11.11 Recognising talented performers in your lessons

Observe a variety of activities. What is it that marks out a talented performer? List the skills they have. What strategies does the teacher use to challenge these pupils?

Finally, be aware of, and sympathetic to, conflicting loyalties. For example, is it appropriate to expect talented pupils to play in a school match if they are preparing for national trials? Furthermore, although they should not usually be isolated from their peers there are occasions when adaptive timetabling is beneficial to them.

SUMMARY

This chapter has highlighted the importance of teaching so that all pupils are able to maximise their learning in physical education. This does not mean treating all pupils the same, but being able to take account of their needs in as inclusive a way as possible. It is a challenging task for inexperienced teachers to learn about each pupil and how best to work with them, but in this chapter we have explained how to identify pupil differences and to plan and deliver lessons so that each pupil's needs are met and their learning maximised. This includes gifted and talented pupils who require additional opportunities within and beyond school curriculum time in order to maximise their considerable potential in physical activity.

FURTHER READING

Read the Sex Discrimination Act (1975), the Education Reform Act (ERA) (1988), the Special Needs and Disability Act (2001), the Revised SEN Code of Practice (DfES, 2001b) and the Race Relations (Amendment) Act (2000) to recognise the significance of these Acts in relation to the statutory entitlement of all pupils.

Key texts

Evans, J. (ed.) (1993) *Equality, Education and Physical Education*, London: Falmer Press. This text examines two central concepts: 'equality' and 'equity'. It is invaluable in supporting physical education teachers' delivery of 'inclusive' teaching and learning in the National Curriculum.

Hayes, S. and Stidder, G. (eds) (2003) *Equity and Inclusion in Physical Education and Sport*, London: Routledge. This text examines issues surrounding 'equity' and 'inclusion'. Concepts such as 'social class', 'gender' and 'physical (dis)ability' are examined and examples of good practice in 'inclusive practice' in physical education and sport are considered.

Other recommended readings

DfES (Department for Education and Skills) (2002) *Key Stage 3 National Strategy, Access and Engagement in Physical Education*, London: HMSO.

DfES (Department for Education and Skills) (2003) Success for All – An Inclusive Approach to Physical Education and Sport. A CD-ROM available from dfes@prolog.uk.com

Runnymede Trust (2003) *Complementing Teachers: A Practical Guide to Promoting Race Equality in Schools*, London: Granada

Chapter 12 Assessing pupils' learning

JEAN O'NEILL AND DANNY OCKMORE

INTRODUCTION

Assessing pupils' learning is an integral part of teaching and learning rather than something 'extra' to do. It is crucial to include assessment-related aspects in all unit and lesson planning even if you are only teaching a few lessons. This chapter examines assessment in physical education. It includes a section on lesson planning and delivery, as the strategies you use for assessing pupils' learning must be included as an integral part of both planning and delivery.

By the end of this chapter you should be able to:

- explain the importance of assessing pupils' learning and understand the relationship between the assessment 'for' and the assessment 'of' learning;
- assess pupils' learning in relation to the learning outcomes in each lesson;
- use this information to plan for pupils' learning in subsequent lessons to maximise the attainment of all pupils;
- maintain records of pupil learning arising from assessment 'for' and 'of' learning.

ASSESSMENT FOR LEARNING OR ASSESSMENT OF LEARNING?

As a teacher you need to assess *for* learning and to assess learning. By assessing pupils' learning in a planned, systematic way in lessons you can feed information into the planning of the next lesson with the aim of challenging pupils to improve their learning. Thus, a continuous cycle occurs because assessment always informs the planning and delivery of your next lesson.

First, let us examine 'assessment *for* learning'. What is assessment for learning? It is 'the process of seeking and interpreting evidence for use by learners and their teachers to decide where the learners are in their learning, where they need to go and how best to get there' (Assessment Reform Group (2002), cited in Department for Education and Skills (DfES), 2004: 5). There are ten principles underpinning assessment for learning. These are:

1   It should be part of the effective planning of teaching and learning.
2   It should focus on how pupils learn.
3   It should be seen as central to teaching.
4   It is a key professional skill for teachers.
5   It should be sensitive and constructive (not negative) because all assessment has an emotional impact on the learners.
6   It should recognise and encourage motivation in learners.

7   It should promote a commitment to the learning goals/targets and a shared knowledge (between the teacher and the learners) of the criteria by which those goals/targets are assessed.

8   As a result of assessment the learners should receive helpful guidance about how to improve.

9   It develops the learners' ability and motivation for self-assessment; which leads to self management and reflection.

10   It should recognise the full range of the achievements of all learners.

(*Source*: Qualifications and Curriculum Authority (QCA) website on assessment for learning)

It should be clear that assessment for learning is a process which uses ongoing assessment of pupils' learning to raise their achievement. It is based on the principle that pupils improve most if they understand what they are aiming to learn and how they go about it. Clearly this must involve careful planning and teaching (see Activities 12.1 and 12.2).

Second, what is the 'assessment *of* learning?' It is a summative assessment as it 'summarises' pupil learning at the end of a period of time; usually a lesson, a unit, a year, or a key stage. A very important aspect of assessment in schools is the formative use of summative data. 'Teachers can use information gained through summative assessment formatively, in order to draw pupils into the assessment process, help pupils understand . . . improve motivation . . . develop independence, enhance target setting . . . increase pupils' understanding and raise . . . standards' (DfES, 2004: 2).

Another question: What summative assessment needs to go into a lesson evaluation so that it can be used formatively i.e. in the next lesson? As a teacher you need to be able to *justify comments you make about the pupils' learning* after a lesson; otherwise you will have insufficient information with which to plan the next lesson's learning outcomes. Answers later!

PLANNING FOR THE ASSESSMENT OF AND FOR PUPILS' LEARNING

Teachers *must* be able to plan lessons so that the differentiated learning outcomes are *clear*, *concise* and *easily assessed*. Furthermore the tasks set in the lesson must relate specifically to the learning outcomes. Joanne is an NQT. Here is Joanne's example for a first netball lesson with a Year 7 class:

What are the learning outcomes (i.e. what all of the pupils should have learnt by the end of the lesson)? By the end of the lesson, pupils will be able to do the following:

1   understand the nature of the game of netball and some basic rules and know that netball is part of the invasion games category;

2   demonstrate the three phases of basic passing in closed practice situations;

3   understand that in certain situations one type of pass is better to use than any others.

These learning outcomes can be differentiated by grouping pupils into (say) three broad 'ability' bands – as it would be very difficult to differentiate a task for each pupil! Joanne has identified three ability bands: 'most', 'some' (least able) and 'a few' (most able). Obviously, Joanne then has to include tasks in the lesson which enable all pupils to achieve the learning outcomes. Differentiated tasks are used, where appropriate to achieve this.

There are different ways of writing learning outcomes. In Chapter 6 learning outcomes are written for the whole class, and it is against these that differentiation in pupil achievement occurs. If learning outcomes are written like this on your course you may want to try to rewrite the learning outcomes in this chapter. For example see Table 12.1, p. 137).

Activity 12.1   Are you assessing pupils' learning systematically?

Look at a specific series of lesson plans for one unit you have taught. Remember that you must include all of the pupils in assessment for learning. The basic strategy to use follows (below). Tick whether you are doing it in your planning and teaching:

1   In your lesson plans do you write *clear, concise* learning outcomes (if these are differentiated for each ability band, do they reflect the different ability bands in the class, e.g. 'top', 'middle' and 'bottom')?

YES   SOMETIMES   NO

Reason for your answer:

How could you improve this work?

2   Do your learning outcomes relate *specifically* to the four strands of the Physical Education National Curriculum *across the unit*; but not necessarily in every lesson?

YES   SOMETIMES   NO

Reason for your answer:

How could you improve this work?

3   You assess pupils' learning against the learning outcomes of the lesson plan. At the start of every lesson do you explain what these are to the class?

YES   SOMETIMES   NO

Reason for your answer:

How could you improve this work?

4　You should engage all pupils in their learning, therefore they all need to understand *what* they are trying to learn and *how* they are going to achieve it (target setting). Do you involve them in this way?

　　YES　　SOMETIMES　　NO

　　Reason for your answer:

　　How could you improve this work?

5　As the pupils are working on tasks do they receive *constructive feedback* about how to improve (from *you, others in the class and/or from themselves*)?

　　YES　　SOMETIMES　　NO

　　Reason for your answer:

　　How can you encourage the latter two sources to engage them in their learning?

6　At the end of the lesson do you review the 'results' with all of the pupils? To what extent did they achieve the learning outcomes? What should they learn in the next lesson?

　　YES　　SOMETIMES　　NO

　　Reason for your answer:

　　How could you improve this work?

Activity 12.2   Using the basic strategy for assessment for learning

You should now be aware of the extent to which you are planning and using assessment for learning in your lessons.

Using the information gathered for Activity 12.1, write a lesson plan that addresses 1–3, then teach the lesson to incorporate 4–6. After the lesson, complete Activity 12.1 again. Has your handling of the basic strategy improved now? If not, why not? How are you going to change this in the next lesson? If your handling of the basic strategy has improved, then repeat Activity 12.1 in another physical education activity.

When you are pleased with your planning and teaching for assessment for learning, read the 10 principles again. You should feel that you are now addressing these more effectively too!

Table 12.1 Learning outcomes and differentiation

Learning outcomes	Differentiation (into three bands, i.e. 'most', 'some' or a 'few' pupils)		
1	After completing this lesson, *most* pupils will . . .	After completing this lesson, *some* pupils will not have made so much progress and will . . .	After completing this lesson a *few* pupils will have progressed further and will . . .
	understand that netball is a non-contact invasion game; play within the court boundaries and usually throw/catch within the footwork rule	understand that netball is a non-contact invasion game; move within court boundaries and show some ability to throw/catch the ball within the footwork rule	understand the nature of the game of netball; be able to throw/catch within the court boundaries and within the footwork rule; using changes of speed to surprise opponents
2	be able to throw to another player standing and while moving and in so doing show preparation, execution and follow through	be able to throw to another player while standing and include at least two of the three passing phases	be able to consistently and accurately throw to another player showing fluent phasing within throwing actions and effective weight transference
3	be able to choose the most effective pass in at least 4 of the 6 examples given and do so after trial and error and from working with other players	be able to choose 1 or 2 effective passes from 6 examples given and do so after trial and error and from working with other players	confidently and correctly choose the most effective pass in all 6 examples and do so using previous learning

Now complete Activity 12.3.

All pupils are encouraged to progress in their learning, therefore the numbers in each differentiated band should change over time as more pupils move to a higher band. However, teachers must remember to challenge the top group too! Planning and teaching differentiated tasks enables teachers to maximise each pupil's learning. Read the information on 'differentiated teaching and learning' in Chapter 11 before continuing here.

Look again at the differentiated learning outcomes in Joanne's lesson (see p. 134). Answer the following questions on your own and then compare your answers with someone else's.

1   Which of the four physical education strands is included?

2   Why? Give possible reasons.

3   Choose one of the four strands which is not included and write a possible differentiated learning outcome for that strand.

Learning outcome

Differentiation

After completing this lesson, *most* pupils will . . .	After completing this lesson, *some* pupils will not have made so much progress and . . .	After completing this lesson *a few* pupils will have progressed further and . . .

CHECK! Are the differentiated learning outcomes clear, concise and easily assessed? If they are, you are ready to move on to the next stage – to plan differentiated tasks which address the learning outcomes in the lesson and to write assessment criteria for the learning outcomes.

CRITERIA FOR ASSESSMENT

Teachers need to be clear of the assessment criteria *before teaching a lesson*. At one level the differentiated learning outcomes *are* assessment criteria because they indicate what each of the different ability bands in the class should be able to do. However, for a more detailed assessment of pupils' learning you need to be able to write assessment criteria for each of the differentiated learning outcomes. These criteria are brief and explicit and are usually used as teaching/learning points in lesson task delivery. An example of the identification of assessment criteria for a swimming lesson is found in Capel (2004: 168) (see Activity 12.4).

Before Mark taught the athletics lesson in Activities 12.4–12.6, he would also have known what the assessment criteria were for each of the learning outcomes – otherwise how would he know what to look for during the lesson in order to judge whether or not the pupils were achieving the learning outcomes? Therefore, you should use the assessment criteria to determine the extent of pupils' learning of hurdling by the end of the lesson (assessment *of* learning) (see Activities 12.5–12.7).

EVALUATING YOUR LESSONS

This is a teacher's everyday record of his/her assessment *of* pupils' learning which occurred in relation to the differentiated learning outcomes, together with some information about what to teach in the next lesson (assessment FOR learning).

It includes this summative information:

- individual pupils who 'represent' the different ability bands;
- evidence to show why the learning outcomes were/were not achieved;
- recognition of what to plan for the next lesson in order to *progress* pupils' learning.

Here is an example of a learning outcome, based on Chelsea School documentation:

By the end of the lesson, pupils will be able to do the following:

1   Follow the teacher's step pattern for the rugby dance.
2   Choose and practise some travelling ideas for the rugby dance from a video recording.
3   Recognise and describe the characteristics of rugby players and show them in their dance.

Activity 12.8 gives Mark's evaluation of this learning outcome.

RECORDING PUPILS' LEARNING

By the end of a unit of work you will have a detailed record of the pupils' learning in that activity and a record of their *progress* because you will have engaged in the process of assessment *for* learning. The need for teachers to record pupils' ability to evaluate has resulted in teachers using varied means of assessment and recording. Video material and digital photography are excellent means of recording pupils' learning and therefore are very good ways of playing back performance for evaluative purposes. Therefore across the range of physical activities and by the end of the units of work you should become familiar with using varied methods of assessment and recording. This necessarily includes theoretical content which is assessed and recorded differently from practical work. These components are present in most physical education and dance accredited courses and, as Stidder (2004: 226) explains, the assessment and moderation of practical work particularly, benefit from the use of 'compressed digital images . . . from video or still cameras which can be electronically sent to the awarding body'.

Activity 12.4 Assessing the four strands of the NCPE

Read the learning outcomes for a Year 8 athletics lesson planned by Mark below. Which of the four strands of the NCPE are included here? Why?

Learning Outcomes

By the end of the lesson pupils will be able to:

1   perform a hurdling action after running between hurdles;
2   perform a fast start;
3   evaluate their starting action and explain how they can improve it.

Write the differentiated learning outcomes:

Learning outcomes	Differentiation		
1	After completing this lesson, most pupils will . . .	After completing this lesson, some pupils will not have made so much progress and . . . e.g. Will run slowly, jump up into the air showing high hurdle clearance with an upright body position.	After completing this lesson a few pupils will have progressed further and . . .
2			
3			

Using Mark's lesson, here are assessment criteria for the learning outcome: *'perform a hurdling action after running between hurdles'*. Remember: all the assessment criteria indicate what each learning outcome *should look like:*

- Fast run, take off far from the hurdle. Lead leg 'reaches' into the clearance and arms/legs work in opposition for balanced clearance. Trailing leg is bent and quickly lifted high and round to the side in order to land with weight forwards to continue running as soon as possible.

Write assessment criteria for the second learning outcome:

Write assessment criteria for *'evaluate their starting action and explain how they can improve it'*:

CHECK! Have you written them in a clear, concise way which will enable you to easily look for evidence that the pupils have achieved learning outcome 3? It may help to refer to the programme of study for Key Stage 3 athletics in the NCPE and e.g. level 5 in the attainment target.

Plan the first gymnastics lesson for Class 7G, based on 'balance and travel'. Write learning outcomes, the differentiation for three ability bands and assessment criteria for each of the learning outcomes. Swap your work with someone else's and give each other feedback on it.

Lesson evaluation (partial) of learning outcome 1

> All pupils were able to copy my examples so these were pitched at the correct level. As expected the higher ability pupils observed and copied more accurately than the others, focusing on the head position and detail of the hands (e.g. Hannah, 'few'). Most pupils (Tom), copied the step pattern but fell behind with the timing because their steps were too large. Josie (some) was able to follow the step pattern but found difficulty adding the arms. The tasks were appropriate for this outcome which required pupils to copy given movements, although the higher ability pupils were not always challenged technically.
>
> (Adapted from Chelsea School documentation, 2003)

Learning outcome 2 and learning outcome 3 would each be evaluated too to record what the pupils learnt, together with some supporting evidence.

Plan and teach a lesson. Make sure that you have written learning outcomes – differentiated for three ability groups in your class and assessment criteria for each.

After the lesson write your lesson evaluation:

Read through your evaluation (which is an assessment *of* pupils' learning) and *using only the information that you have written* decide whether or not you would change any of the (differentiated) learning outcomes for the next lesson (assessment *for* learning). Why have you made that decision?

SUMMARY

This chapter enables you to understand how to assess pupils' learning, including managing the interrelationship between summative (assessment of learning) and formative assessment (assessment for learning), particularly when planning and evaluating lessons. Consequently you should realise that the information gained from assessing pupils' learning is used *systematically* by informing the planning and delivery of, for example, the next lesson. Assessment for learning also requires pupils to share the responsibility for lesson delivery and appraisal of their work. This relates well to the strand of 'evaluating and improving' which should feature in the learning outcomes of most physical education lessons. Assessment for learning is central to the National Key Stage 3 Strategy and you are advised to read DfES (2004) to extend your understanding of teaching, learning and integrated assessment.

FURTHER READING

Lockwood, A. and Newton, A. (2004) Assessment in Physical Education, in S. Capel (ed.) *Learning to Teach Physical Education in the Secondary School*, 2nd edn, London: Routledge, pp. 165–84. This highlights the need for the 'assessment' of pupils' learning to be fully integrated into everyday teaching; not included as a 'bolt-on' extra. Consequently, it provides a conceptual understanding of 'assessment' in the National Curriculum together with an insight into 'broad issues and strategies', an understanding of which is crucial for effective practice of teachers and pupils in physical education.

Other useful resources

http://www.qca.org.uk/ages3–14/afl/295.html
http://www.qca.org.uk/ages3–14/afl/296.html
http://www.qca.org.uk/ca/5–14/afl/

A DVD entitled 'Assessment in Physical Education', produced by Claverham Community College, a specialist sports college, is designed to assist students and inexperienced teachers to understand 'assessment' through interactive tasks within practical examples in physical education. It is designed to make 'assessment' accessible and can be used as a 'stand-alone' learning aid and/or as an integral part of your study for this chapter. It includes: 'defining assessment', 'planning for assessment' and 'using assessment information' to inform your teaching. Examples show work in progress from NCPE, the four strands, GCSE Physical Education and GCSE Dance. Copies can be obtained via the school's website: info@ claverham.e-sussex.sch.uk

Part 4 Moving on

Chapter 13 Working with others

JEAN O'NEILL AND KAREN PACK

INTRODUCTION

Our rapidly changing society provides the context in which all teachers work. This development is apparent in education in general and in physical education in particular, not least because over the past few years we have experienced increased politicisation of 'physical education' and 'sport' by central government and therefore by key national sporting agencies.

The physical education teacher is responsible for delivering the physical education curriculum and for teaching in the wider sense (see Chapters 7 and 8 and Zwozdiak-Myers *et al.*, 2004). However, there are now many other 'agencies' and individuals who also have an interest in and a commitment to the physical welfare and development of children and young people and therefore the physical education teacher has also to engage in different roles with different people.

By the end of this chapter, you should be able to:

* recognise the range of roles undertaken by a physical education teacher, including teaching the curriculum, extra-curricular activities and school sport;
* understand why a physical education teacher has these different roles;
* recognise why a physical education teacher works with others and how;
* understand agencies in physical education and sport; how they impact on the physical education curriculum and therefore upon the role of the physical education teacher;
* critically examine some of the issues arising from working with others.

THE PHYSICAL EDUCATION TEACHER'S ROLE

The physical education teacher teaches the physical education curriculum, delivered largely through the National Curriculum for Physical Education (NCPE). This is that part of the provision which is a requirement for all state school pupils which is delivered during the timetabled day. There is 'considerable leeway in relation to the exact nature of the curriculum and the specific focus of the work' (Zwozdiak-Myers *et al.*, 2004: 250), therefore you have to make decisions about the content and how it is taught.

However, the physical education teacher also has responsibility for taking non-compulsory extra-curricular activities – and these are often seen as integral to the role. Extra-curricular activities take place before and/or after the timetabled day as well as during lunch time. The extra-curricular provision in any one school may comprise competitive activities – including inter-school competitions and school teams as well as a range of other non-competitive activities.

Recently, the term 'physical education and school sport' has been used to describe the curriculum and extra-curricular provision within the school.

In particular, extra-curricular activities provide opportunities for pupils to experience 'high quality physical education and school sport', the basic principles of which are to 'enable all young people to take part in and enjoy physical education and sport. It promotes young people's health, safety and well being and enables all young people to improve and achieve in line with their age and potential' (DfES/DCMS, 2004). Indeed, they are an integral part of enabling schools to meet the aim of the national strategy for physical education, school sport and club links (PESSCL) to 'increase the percentage of school children who spend a minimum of two hours each week on high quality physical education and school sport within and beyond the curriculum to 75% by 2006' (DfES/DCMS, 2003) (see Activity 13.1).

Activity 13.1 Physical education and school sport provision

Write down what physical education and school sport consist of in your school or another school with which you are familiar. Go through the physical education department's annual calendar to help you with this activity. Be as thorough as you can as the answers you give will be used in Activity 13.2.

Make notes under the headings:

    during/after the school day
    on-/off-site
    staff involved
    role of the physical education teacher

Who does the physical education teacher work with and/or manage to deliver this range of provision?

Why?

There is a danger that because the media and other agencies such as the Office for Standards in Education (OfSTED) focus on the *national* curriculum, people may over-simplify the work of the physical education teacher by not recognising the different roles that s/he engages in during the timetabled day and extra-curricular activities. Before you read the rest of the chapter you should already be aware that physical education teachers undertake different roles because they deliver the physical education *national curriculum* and extra-curricular activities. You also need to understand that it is diverse because it occurs during and after the school day; on and off school premises and includes staff other than physical education teachers (see Activity 13.2).

Activity 13.2   Working with others in physical education

Read the 'Education' section of the consultation document *Choose Health, Choose Activity* (DoH/DCMS, 2004) and make notes under the headings you used for Activity 13.1.

Who is the physical education teacher going to work with and/or manage in these proposals? Why?

Will the physical education teacher work with more or less people than you noted for Activity 13.1? Why?

Are any of the people identified in this activity working with physical education teachers so closely that they could be called 'partners'?

TEACHING THE PHYSICAL EDUCATION CURRICULUM

All physical education staff have the important role of teaching the physical education curriculum. This includes their leadership role in delivering the NCPE so that all pupils learn through the four strands by experiencing 'breadth of study' – the six areas of activity (see also Chapter 4 and Murdoch, 2004) to enable all pupils to fulfil their full potential. The aims of the National Curriculum permeate all the 'core' and 'foundation' subjects. These aims and the values upon which the National Curriculum is based feature in the content you deliver and how it is presented, and as such are implicit in your teaching of the NCPE's 'breadth of study'. Furthermore, the 'general teaching requirements' (inclusion, use of language, use of information and communications technology (ICT) and health and safety) are delivered through all curriculum subjects. Physical education also contributes to learning across the curriculum in a number of areas such as spiritual, moral, social and cultural development, key skills (communication, application of number, IT, working with others, improving own learning and performance, problem solving) and thinking skills (see Chapters 7 and 8), as well as work-related learning and education for sustainable development.

Therefore in your role as a physical education teacher: you *deliver* the physical education National Curriculum, you speak and act in *support of it*, but as a *reflective practitioner* you also have the enthusiasm and ability to *improve it* – in your school and as a *national* curriculum. Thus, you should critically examine how it could be strengthened (see Activity 13.3).

OTHER INFLUENCES ON THE PHYSICAL EDUCATION CURRICULUM

It is important to recognise that we live in a society in which change rather than the status quo is the norm. The need to change applies equally to you and to the physical education curriculum; hence your need to critically examine the curriculum and consider ways that it can be improved and strengthened. In your role as a custodian of that curriculum you need to be able to recognise opportunities as well as threats. There are other individuals and 'agencies' who would like to influence the teaching of physical education in curriculum time, as well as the NCPE itself. These provide opportunities, but they may also be seen as a threat. You must therefore be aware of what they have to offer, but also of their motives and their relationships with other organisations, including central government. Therefore, although you play a very important role in leading, managing and delivering the physical education curriculum through which every pupil can fulfil their full potential, other people can support

Activity 13.3 The physical education teacher as a defender of the national curriculum

Write down four possible situations in which you may have to *support/defend* the NCPE when working with other people. Give the examples and your response for each.

For example, at a Year 9 parents' evening there are complaints about compulsory dance lessons.

My response: 'Dance has inherent qualities such as expressive movement, which do not feature/feature less in other physical activity areas.'

1   Example ....
    ....
    ....
    ....

    Response ....
    ....
    ....
    ....

2   Example ....
    ....
    ....
    ....

    Response ....
    ....
    ....
    ....

3   Example ....
    ....
    ....
    ....

    Response ....
    ....
    ....
    ....

4   Example ....
    ....
    ....
    ....

    Response ....
    ....
    ....
    ....

its delivery. After all 'the need to be versatile and responsive to current and future trends in the social and political climate which offers physical education to young people is crucial to your professional success' (Shenton and Hepworth, 2004: 264).

WORKING WITH OTHERS

One of the main developments in the provision of physical education, school sport and other extra-curricular activities, as well as physical activities in the community is the need to make full use of resources. These resources include adults who support the delivery of the physical education curriculum, extra-curricular activities and school sport. Pupils with special educational needs may be allocated a Learning Support Assistant (LSA) during physical education lessons. Physical education staff must work closely with LSAs in order to provide inclusive lessons for all pupils. Other adults can also make an important contribution, even though they are not (physical education) teachers. Adults Other than Teachers (AOTTs) make an important contribution to the physical education, school sport and extra-curricular programmes and as such are well placed to provide continuity of delivery for young people through their involvement in community-based programmes as well. AOTTs include coaches and choreographers who feature in school-based and out-of-school sporting and dance programmes.

BEYOND THE PHYSICAL EDUCATION CURRICULUM – PROVIDING EXTRA-CURRICULAR ACTIVITY AND SUPPORTING OUT-OF-SCHOOL PARTICIPATION IN SPORT AND DANCE

The *extra-curricular* physical education programme should be designed to help pupils develop their interests and expertise – many of which stem from their physical education experiences during the timetabled day. For those pupils who have particular expertise, an emerging talent or a particular interest, a physical education teacher's role also includes supporting young people's sporting and dance experiences outside school and in the community (see, for example, Shenton and Hepworth, 2004). Competitive experiences such as house matches and other experiences such as creating productions in dance, for example, function as higher levels of challenge for pupils and in so doing provide a 'bridge' between school-based physical education and sporting and dance opportunities in the community. Given that physical education has a wide breadth of study and seeks to enable each pupil to fulfil his/her potential, it follows that the breadth of the extra-curricular programme and its synchronisation with community sport and dance opportunities are equally broad and require more staffing than physical education teachers could possibly manage themselves. It also means that physical education teachers should know about the opportunities in their locality and are able to advise pupils accordingly. Therefore, the physical education curriculum is led and (largely) delivered by physical education teachers, whereas the latter must work more in *partnership* with other contributors to deliver out of school activities (see Activity 13.4).

RECENT PHYSICAL EDUCATION AND SCHOOL SPORT 'INITIATIVES'

There are many government initiatives which relate to and/or impact on physical education teachers. Three initiatives are included in Activities 13.5, 13.6, 13.7 and 13.8. These are at the 'cutting edge' of its plan for physical education and sport (DfES/DCMS, 2004). It is important to note that the role of the physical education teacher itself has been redefined for some staff who work in Specialist Sports Colleges and in the School Sport Partnerships Programme (SSPP) (see Activities 13.5 and 13.6).

The physical education teachers' management of additional support workers is crucial to the smooth operation of a SSPP. The LSAs, AOTTs and other volunteers undergo training

1   Use the information you obtained in Activity 13.1 to examine in more detail who the physical education teacher works with and why. Select eight contrasting examples.

Activity	Location (in/out of school)	Organised by	Delivered by	Reasons for
Swimming gala	In school	PE teachers	PE teachers, parents, life guards	Expertise

2   List below the people with whom physical education teachers work to provide sport and dance opportunities for young people, in the community. Refer to Activity 13.1 to complete the list.

3   Which of the opportunities in 2 also support the NCPE areas? Why do they do this and how?

Activity 13.5 Specialist sports colleges (SSCs)

Visit the Specialist Schools information website at www.standards.dfes.gov.uk/ specialistschools and the Youth Sport Trust website www.youthsporttrust.org. What are the purposes of specialist schools and how do these purposes apply specifically to SSCs? Now answer the questions below:

- What are the main aims of an SSC?

- What are the roles of the Head of Physical Education and the Director of Sport, and how do they work with AOTTs?

The case study example in the Appendix explains how these roles operate in one SSC.

Activity 13.6 School sport partnerships programme (SSPP)

Tessa Jowell, the Secretary of State for Culture, Media and Sport said in 2004 that:

> [there is] . . . evidence of the difference that the School Sport Partnerships Programme is making. Our target that 3 out of 4 of all children will participate in at least two hours high quality physical education and school sport per week as a minimum by 2006 is well within reach.
>
> (Teachernet.gov.uk/teachingandlearning/subjects /pe/penews/newsimpact/ Accessed 15.4.04)

1   Access the teachernet website as well as the OfSTED website (http://www. Ofsted.gov.uk) to find out what the 'evidence' is for this statement. Now access the Youth Sport Trust (YST) website. What is a School Sport Coordinator (SSCo) and what is their role in an SSPP? Then answer the question. You need to think carefully before writing your answer.

Question: All SSCos are physical education teachers. Suggest what they could do when working alongside other physical education teachers in their 'family' of schools to achieve 'high quality' physical education in Key Stages 2 and 3. What difficulties could occur? Suggest how they might be overcome.

2   After answering the question discuss your answers with an SSCo.
3   Also ask the SSCo to tell you who the physical education staff work with and why. Do these include, for example, AOTT, LSA, Sports Development Officer (SDO), dance animateur, etc.?

The case study example in the Appendix includes information from one SSC. For more information on the SSCo's role e-mail ystinfo@lboro.ac.uk.

and quality assurance procedures so that pupils' learning is maximised and the adults understand related matters such as child protection and entitlement. Therefore physical education teachers must know how to access the information which supports the professional development of the people they work closely with in pursuit of high quality physical education.

PHYSICAL EDUCATION, SCHOOL SPORT AND CLUB LINKS (PESSCLs)

Arguably no other government physical education and school sport initiative demonstrates the need for physical education teachers to work with other personnel as the PESSCL strategy. As an 'umbrella' initiative conceived and managed by two government departments (DfES and DCMS), it embraces the SSC and SSPP as key strands (see Activities 13.7 and 13.8)

Activity 13.7   Agencies that support the professional development of support staff

Access three websites below to read about how these agencies provide support to physical education teachers seeking to improve the professional development of others:

Sport England: www.sportengland.org/active_schools or contact the Active Schools Helpline: 0800 169 2299 to find about the Active Schools programme.

Youth Sport Trust (YST): www.youthsporttrust.org

Sports Coach UK: www.sportscoachuk.org

Activity 13.8   Working with others in *partnership*

Read about the PESSCL strategy either online at www.dfes.gov.uk/pess or www.culture.gov.uk or in hard copy (DfES/DCMS, 2003). Note the central theme of 'partnerships' and 'working together'. Also note the inclusion of 'high quality' physical education and the *necessity* for physical education teachers to work with others in order to improve pupil performance.

SUMMARY

In summary, it should be clear to you that physical education teachers have a multi-faceted role – part of which can be attributed to the growth in agencies (including the government), who also have an interest in the physical well-being of children and young people. Such has been the rapid development of this interest that it is now considered to be a necessary part of the physical education teacher's role to work with other adults in as effective a way as possible in order to bring about and maintain high quality physical education and in so doing to promote young people's continued participation in sport and dance in extra-curricular activities, outside school and after they have left school. Furthermore, it is indicative of the increased specialisation and frequency of this work with others that different career opportunities have been created for physical education teachers – particularly those who work in SSCs and SSPP.

APPENDIX TO CHAPTER 13

First, access the 'school sport partnerships programme' website www. youthsporttrust.org to read about the roles of the partnership link teacher (PLTs), specialist link teacher (SLT), partnership development manager (PDM) and school sport coordinator (SSCo).

Case study example for Activities 13.5 and 13.6; from Coopers Company and Coborn school, a Specialist Sports College in Essex

The physical education staff are led by the Head of Physical Education (HoPE) who works alongside the Director of Sport. The HoPE manages, monitors and develops the physical education curriculum and the extracurricular programme. He also manages the staff within the department and ensures that they all have a comprehensive programme of Continuing Professional Development (CPD), through which he monitors their performance targets. He liaises with the Director of Sport to raise the standards of physical education and sport within the school, by improving the quality of teaching and learning. The HoPE is also responsible for the completion of aspects of the Sports College Plan.

The Director of Sport oversees the development of the school as a successful and effective Sports College. She manages the Sports College management team and works with designated post holders to ensure the successful implementation of the Plan. Additionally she works closely with the Youth Sport Trust (YST) in developing new initiatives and promoting their involvement in case studies and Sports College research projects. The Director of Sport is on the school's leadership team and is tasked to deliver whole school impact through the Sports College Plan.

The School Sport Partnerships Programme (SSPP) includes Coopers Company and Coborn school and its family of schools. This family consists of Coopers Company and Coborn school as the 'hub-site' and seven other partner secondary schools which have between them 38 partner primary schools.

Clearly, in such a large structure, communication is essential. Sound management of the family of schools by the Partnership Development Manager (PDM) is essential to the smooth running of the scheme. The PDM is an effective communicator who works closely with headteachers, SSCos, PLTs, pupils and parents. She has highly refined organisational skills and is an advocate of the wider values of physical activity.

Communication is via weekly timetabled meetings with the SSCos. This is an essential part of quality assurance and a highly effective way to monitor and evaluate work which is taking place and which features in the partnership development Plan. Termly meetings with a steering group which consists of the PDM, the YST's area support officer, senior County Education representatives, the county Sports Development Officer (SDO), the County Finance Officer, primary and secondary heads, representatives from both the SSCos and PLTs, together with the Director of Sport are designed to ensure accountability and to promote open communication. In the family of schools the SSCos are a vital part as they must work closely with their family and with their 'own' PLTs. They all receive national training and have a local programme of CPD. An important feature of a good SSCo is their ability to form a good working relationship with the primary headteachers by paying regular visits to all the primary schools in their part of the family.

An annual review is written by the PDM and accompanied by a data collection process; this monitors the impact of the Plan and is used to generate good practice examples that can be shared nationally.

However well this group of staff works together, they have to have the support of others in order to pursue the objectives of the SSPP particularly. The physical education department is at the centre of this delivery and between them have the expertise to deliver a broad and balanced National Curriculum, together with an extra-curricular programme to which all pupils have access. Additionally the partnership (as with all partnerships) receive New Opportunities Funding (NOF), which enables out-of-hours learning (OOHL) activities to be developed. These are designed to enhance the opportunities for young people and include after school but also enrichment clubs before school and during lunchtimes. The funding may be used to purchase equipment or to pay coaches and other AOTTs to deliver aspects of the plan.

The management of additional support workers is crucial to the smooth operation of the SSPP. Within the Sports College framework the responsibility for LSAs, AOTTs and volunteers is that of the Community Liaison Officer.

The Sports College works closely with the County SDO to ensure that the objectives of the partnership work in harmony with the County Sports Strategy. The SDO also creates a database of coaches and their qualifications for people to access. During periods of consultation a timetable of coaching courses is discussed which ensures that the courses are open to as many of the appropriate people as possible in the local community.

Now find out how another SSC and SSPP works and compare this to the case study above.

Bibliography

Abbott, J. and Ryan, T. (2000) *The Unfinished Revolution: Learning, Human Behaviour, Community and Political Paradox*, Stafford: Network Educational Press Ltd.

Arnold, P.J. (1988) *Education, Movement and the Curriculum*, London: The Falmer Press.

Assessment Reform Group (1999) *Assessment for Learning: Beyond the Black Box*, Cambridge: University of Cambridge, Faculty of Education.

Ayres, H. and Gray, F. (1998) *Classroom Management: A Practical Approach for Primary and Secondary Teachers*, London: David Fulton.

BAALPE (British Association of Advisers and Lecturers in Physical Education) (2004) *Safe Practice in Physical Education and School Sport*, Leeds: Coachwise Solutions.

Baumann, A., Bloomfield, A. and Roughton, L. (1997) *Becoming a Secondary School Teacher* London: Hodder and Stoughton.

Beedy, J.P. (1997) *Sports Plus: Positive Learning Using Sports*, Hamilton: Project Adventure.

Bell, J. (1999) *Doing Your Research Project. A Guide for First-Time Researchers in Education and Social Science*, 3rd edn, Buckingham: Open University Press.

Bentley, T. and Gardner, H. (1998) *Learning Beyond the Classroom: Education for a Changing World*, London: RoutledgeFalmer.

Benyon, L. (1981) Curriculum continuity, *Education 3–13*, 9(2): 36–41.

Bleach, K. (2000) *The Newly Qualified Secondary Teachers Handbook: Meeting the Standards in Secondary and Middle Schools*, London: David Fulton.

Boud, D., Keogh, R. and Walker, D. (eds) (1985) *Reflection: Turning Experience into Learning*, London: Kogan Page.

Bryson, J. (1998) *Effective Classroom Management*, London: Hodder and Stoughton.

Capel, S. (ed.) (1997) *Learning to Teach Physical Education in the Secondary School: A Companion to School Experience*, London: Routledge.

Capel, S. (ed.) (2004) *Learning to Teach Physical Education in the Secondary School: A Companion to School Experience*, 2nd edn, London: Routledge.

Capel, S., Leask, M. and Turner, T. (eds) (1999) *Learning to Teach in the Secondary School: A Companion to School Experience*, 2nd edn, London: Routledge.

Capel, S., Leask, M. and Turner, T. (eds) (2001) *Learning to Teach in the Secondary School: A Companion to School Experience*, 3rd edn, London: Routledge.

Capel, S., Leask, M. and Turner, T. (eds) (2005) *Learning to Teach in the Secondary School: A Companion to School Experience*, 4th edn, London: Routledge.

Capel, S. and Piotrowski, S. (eds) (2001) *Issues in Physical Education*, London: RoutledgeFalmer.

Capel, S., Whitehead, M. and Zwozdiak-Myers, P. (2004) Developing and maintaining an effective learning environment, in S. Capel (ed.) *Learning to Teach Physical Education in the Secondary School: A Companion to School Experience*, 2nd edn, London: Routledge, pp. 102–19.

Carr, W. and Kemmis, S. (1986) *Becoming Critical: Education, Knowledge and Action Research*, Lewes: Falmer.

Chelsea School (2003) *Good Practice Pack, School Experience*, Eastbourne: University of Brighton.

Cohen, L., Manion, L. and Morrison, K. (2004) *A Guide to Teaching Practice*, 3rd edn, London: Routledge.

Croner (2004) *The Head's Legal Guide*, Kingston upon Thames: WoltersKluwer.

DCMS (Department for Culture, Media and Sport) (2000) *A Sporting Future for All*, London: DCMS.

DES (Department of Education and Science) (1987) *The Curriculum from 5 to 16: Curriculum Matters 2*, London: HMSO.

DES (Department of Education and Science) (1988) *The Education Reform Act*, London: HMSO.

DES (Department of Education and Science) (1991) *Physical Education for Ages 5–16: Proposals of the Secretary of State for Education and Science and the Secretary of State for Wales*, London: HMSO.

DES (Department of Education and Science) (1992) *The Education (Schools) Act*, London: HMSO.

DES/WO (Department of Education and Science and the Welsh Office) (1991) *Physical Education for Ages 5–16: Final Report of the National Curriculum Physical Education Working Group*, London: HMSO.

Dewey, J. (1933) *How We Think*, New York: Heath and Co.

DfE (Department for Education) (1994) *The Education of Children with Emotional and Behavioural Difficulties*, Circular 9/94, London: DfE.

DfEE/QCA (Department for Education and Employment/Qualifications and Curriculum Authority) (1999) *Physical Education: The National Curriculum for England*, London: HMSO.

DfEE/TTA (Department for Education and Employment/Teacher Training Agency) (2004) *Qualifying to Teach: Professional Standards for Qualified Teacher Status and Requirements for Initial Teacher Training*, London: TTA.

DfES (Department for Education and Skills) (2001a) *Statistics of Education: Special Educational Needs in England*, January, Circular 12/01, London: HMSO.

DfES (Department for Education and Skills) (2001b) *Special Educational Needs Code of Practice*, London: HMSO.

DfES (Department for Education and Skills) (2002) *Key Stage 3 National Strategy, Access and Engagement in Physical Education*, London: HMSO.

DfES (Department for Education and Skills) (2003) Success for All: An Inclusive Approach to Physical Education and Sport, CD-ROM available from dfes@prolog.uk.com

DfES (Department for Education and Skills) (2004) *Key Stage 3 National Strategy, Assessment for Learning*, London: HMSO.

DfES/DCMS (Department for Education and Skills/Department for Culture, Media and Sport) (2003) *Learning through Physical Education and Sport*, London: HMSO.

DfES/DCMS (Department for Education and Skills/Department for Culture, Media and Sport) (2004) *High Quality PE and Sport for Young People*, London: HMSO.

DNH (Department of National Heritage) (1995) *Sport: Raising the Game*, London: HMSO.

DoH/DCMS (Department of Health/Department for Culture, Media and Sport) (2004) *Choose Health, Choose Activity: A Consultation Document*, London: DoH/DCMS.

Donovan, G., McNamara, J. and Gianoli, P. (1988) *Exercise Danger*, Floreat Park: Wellness Australia.

Ebbutt, D. (1985) Educational action research: Some general concerns and specific quibbles, in R. Burgess (ed.) *Issues in Educational Research*, Lewes: Falmer Press.

Elliott, J. (1991) *Action Research for Educational Change*, Buckingham: Open University Press.

Evans, J. (ed.) (1993) *Equality, Education and Physical Education*, London: Falmer Press.

Gardner, H. (1993) *Frames of Mind: Multiple Intelligences*, London: HarperCollins.

Garner, P. (2005) Behaviour for learning: a positive approach to managing classroom behaviour, in S. Capel, M. Leask and T. Turner (eds) *Learning to Teach in the Secondary School: A Companion to School Experience*, 4th edn, London: RoutledgeFalmer, pp. 136–50.

Griffey, D.C. and Housner, L.D. (1999) Teacher thinking and decision making in physical education: Planning, perceiving, and implementing instruction, in C. Hardy and M. Mawer (eds) *Learning and Teaching in Physical Education*, London: Falmer Press.

Grimmett, P. and Erickson, G. (1988) *Reflection in Teacher Education*, New York: Teachers College Press.

Hargreaves, A., Earl, L., Moore, S. and Manning, S. (2001) *Learning to Change: Teaching Beyond Subjects and Standards*, San Francisco: Jossey-Bass.

Harris, J. (1996) *Health-Related Exercise in the National Curriculum: Key Stages 1 to 4*, Leeds: Human Kinetics.

Harris, J. and Elbourn, J. (1997) *Teaching Health-Related Exercise at Key Stages 1 and 2*, Leeds: Human Kinetics.

Harris, J. and Elbourn, J. (2002) *Warming Up and Cooling Down*, Leeds: Human Kinetics.

Hayes, S. and Stidder, G. (eds) (2003) *Equity and Inclusion in Physical Education and Sport*, London: Routledge.

Health and Safety Executive (1999) *Five Steps to Risk Assessment*, Sudbury: Health and Safety Executive.

Her Majesty's Inspectorate (HMI) (1987) *Quality in Schools: The Initial Training of Teachers*, London: HMSO.

Hopkins, D. (2002) *A Teacher's Guide to Classroom Research*, 3rd edn, Maidenhead: Open University Press.

Hopper, B., Grey, J. and Maude, P. (2003) *Teaching Physical Education in the Primary School*, London: RoutledgeFalmer.

Katene, W. (2004) Continuing professional development in PE, in S. Capel (ed.) *Learning to Teach Physical Education in the Secondary School: A Companion to School Experience*, 2nd edn, London: RoutledgeFalmer, pp. 301–16.

Katene, W. and Edmondson, G. (2004) Teaching safely and safety in PE, in S. Capel (ed.) *Learning to Teach Physical Education in the Secondary School: A Companion to School Experience*, 2nd edn, London: RoutledgeFalmer, pp. 120–40.

Kemmis, S. (1988) Action research in retrospect and prospect, in Deakin University, *The Action Research Reader*, Victoria: Deakin University Press.

Kolb, D. (1984) *Experiential Learning*, Englewood Cliffs, NJ: Prentice-Hall.

Kyriacou, C. (1998) *Essential Teaching Skills*, 2nd edn, London: Stanley Thornes.

Laker, A. (2001) *Developing Personal, Social and Moral Education through Physical Education*, London: RoutledgeFalmer.

Lawrence, J., Capel, S. and Whitehead, M. (2004) Lesson organisation and management, in S. Capel (ed.) *Learning to Teach Physical Education in the Secondary School: A Companion to School Experience*, 2nd edn, London: RoutledgeFalmer, pp. 82–97.

Lawrence, J., Taylor, A. and Capel, S. (2005) Developing further as a teacher, in S. Capel, M. Leask and T. Turner (eds) *Learning to Teach in the Secondary School: A Companion to School Experience*, 4th edn, London: RoutledgeFalmer, pp. 412–22.

Leah, J. and Capel, S. (2000) Competition and co-operation in physical education, in S. Capel and S. Piotrowski (eds) *Issues in Physical Education*, London: RoutledgeFalmer, pp. 144–58.

Leask, M. (2001) Improving your teaching: an introduction to action research and reflective practice, in S. Capel, M. Leask and T. Turner (eds) *Learning to Teach in the Secondary School: A Companion to School Experience*, 3rd edn, London: RoutledgeFalmer, pp. 278–85.

Leask, M. (2005) Becoming a teacher in S. Capel, M. Leask and T. Turner (eds) *Learning to Teach in the Secondary School: A Companion to School Experience*, 4th edn, London: Routledge, pp. 5, 6.

Lockwood, A. and Newton, A. (2004) Assessment in Physical Education, in S. Capel (ed.) *Learning to Teach Physical Education in the Secondary School: A Companion to School Experience*, 2nd edn, London: Routledge, pp. 165–84.

Loughran, J. (1996) *Developing Reflective Practice: Learning about Teaching and Learning through Modelling*, London: Falmer Press.

Macintyre, C. (2000) *The Art of Action Research in the Classroom*, London: David Fulton.

McKernan, J. (1996) *Curriculum Action Research*, 2nd edn, London: Kogan Page.

Moore, A. (2000) *Teaching and Learning: Pedagogy, Curriculum and Culture*, London: RoutledgeFalmer.

Mosston, M. and Ashworth, S. (2002) *Teaching Physical Education*, 5th edn, San Francisco: Benjamin Cummings.

Murdoch, E. (1997) The background to, and developments from, the National Curriculum for PE, in S. Capel (ed.) *Learning to Teach Physical Education in the Secondary School: A Companion to School Experience*, London: RoutledgeFalmer, pp. 252–70.

Murdoch, E. (2004) NCPE 2000 – Where are we so far?, in S. Capel (ed.) *Learning to Teach Physical Education in the Secondary School: A Companion to School Experience*, 2nd edn. London: RoutledgeFalmer, pp. 280–300.

(NCET) National Council for Educational Technology (1993) Differing differentiation, in *Differentiating the School Curriculum*, Wiltshire: Wiltshire LEA.

Norris, C.M. (1999) *The Complete Guide to Stretching*, London: A&C Black.

OfSTED (Office for Standards in Education) (2002) *Secondary Inspection Reports 2000/01 Physical Education*, London: HMSO.

OfSTED (Office for Standards in Education) (2003*) Secondary Initial Teacher Training: Secondary Physical Education Subject Inspection Reports 1999–2003*, London: Oxford

OfSTED/TTA (Office for Standards in Education/Teacher Training Agency) (1997/98) *Framework for the Assessment of Quality and Standards in Initial Teacher Training* (Revised), London: OFSTED.

PEAUK (2000–present) Physical Education and the law, *The British Journal of Teaching Physical Education*, vol. 31 onwards.

Penney, D. (2001) The revision and initial implementation of the National Curriculum for Physical Education in England, *Bulletin of Physical Education*, 37(2): 93–134.

Penney, D. and Chandler, T. (2000) A curriculum with connections?, *The British Journal of Teaching Physical Education*, 31(2): 37–40.

Penney, D. and Evans, J. (2000) Dictating the play: direction in physical education and sport policy development in England and Wales, in K. Green and K. Hardman (eds) *Physical Education: A Reader*, Oxford: Meyer and Meyer Sport.

Pollard, A. (2002) *Reflective Teaching: Effective and Evidence-informed Professional Practice*, London: Continuum.

Pollard, A. and Triggs, P. (1997) *Reflective Teaching in the Secondary School*, London: Cassell.

Raymond, C. (ed.) (1999) *Safety Across the Curriculum*, London: RoutledgeFalmer.

Rink, J.E. (1999) Instruction from a learning perspective, in C. Hardy and M. Mawer (eds) *Learning and Teaching in Physical Education*, London: Falmer Press.

Robson, C. (1993) *Real World Research. A Resource for Social Scientists and Practitioner-Researchers*, Oxford: Blackwell.

Rose, C. (1985) *Accelerated Learning*, Aylesbury: Accelerated Learning Systems Ltd.

Runnymede Trust (2003) *Complementing Teachers: A Practical Guide to Promoting Race Equality in Schools*, London: Granada Learning.

Russell, T. and Munby, H. (1992) *Teachers and Teaching: From Classroom to Reflection*, London: Falmer Press.

Schön, D. (1983) *The Reflective Practitioner: How Professionals Think in Action*, New York: Basic Books.

Severs, J., Whitlam, P. and Woodhouse, J. (2003) *Safety and Risk in Primary School Physical Education: A Guide for Teachers*, London: Routledge.

Shenton, P. and Hepworth, N. (2004) From school to community: physical education beyond the classroom, in S. Capel (ed.) *Learning to Teach Physical Education in the Secondary School: A Companion to School Experience*, 2nd edn, London: RoutledgeFalmer, pp. 259–79.

Siedentop, D., Tousignant, M. and Parker, M. (1982) *Academic Learning Time: Physical Education Coaching Manual*, Columbus, OH: School of Health, Physical Education and Recreation.

Stidder, G. (2004) The use of information and communications technology (ICT) in PE, in S. Capel (ed.) *Learning to Teach Physical Education in the Secondary School: A Companion to School Experience*, 2nd edn, London: RoutledgeFalmer, pp. 219–38.

Talbot, M. (1993) Physical Education and the National Curriculum: some political issues, in G. McFee and A. Tomlinson (eds) *Education, Sport and Leisure: Connections and Controversies*, Brighton: University of Brighton, pp. 34–65.

Taylor, A., Lawrence, J. and Capel, S. (2005) Getting your first post, in S. Capel, M. Leask and T. Turner (eds) *Learning to Teach in the Secondary School: A Companion to School Experience*, 4th edn, London: RoutledgeFalmer, pp. 396–411.

Theodoulides, A. (2003) 'I would never personally tell anyone to break the rules, but you can bend them': teaching moral values through team games, *European Journal of Physical Education*, 8(2): 141–59.

TTA (Teacher Training Agency) (2003) *Career Entry and Development Profile: Maintaining a Professional Portfolio*, London: TTA.

TTA/DfES (Teacher Training Agency/Department for Education and Skills) (2002) *Qualifying to Teach: Professional Standards for Qualified Teacher Status and Requirements for Initial Teacher Training*, London: TTA.

Vickerman, P. (2004) Planning for an inclusive approach to your teaching, in S. Capel (ed.) *Learning to Teach Physical Education in the Secondary School: A Companion to School Experience*, 2nd edn, London: RoutledgeFalmer, pp. 153–64.

Weare, K. (2004) *Developing the Emotionally Literate School*, London: Paul Chapman Publishing.

Whitehead, M. (2000) Aims as an issue in physical education, in S. Capel and S. Piotrowski (eds) *Issues in Physical Education*, London: RoutledgeFalmer, pp. 7–21.

Whitehead, M. (2004) Aims of PE, in S. Capel (ed.) *Learning to Teach Physical Education in the Secondary School: A Companion to School Experience*, 2nd edn, London: RoutlegdeFalmer, pp. 17–26.

Whitehead, M. with Zwozdiak-Myers, P. (2004) Designing teaching approaches to achieve intended learning outcomes, in S. Capel (ed.) *Learning to Teach Physical Education in the Secondary School: A Companion to School Experience*, 2nd edn, London: RoutledgeFalmer, pp. 141–52.

Whitlam, P. (2003) Risk management principles in J. Severs, P. Whitlam and J. Woodhouse (eds) *Safety and Risk in Primary School Physical Education: A Guide for Teachers*, London: Routledge.

Whitlam, P. (2004) *Case Law in Physical Education and School Sport*, Leeds: Coachwise Solutions.

Zwozdiak-Myers, P., Whitehead, M. and Capel, S. (2004) Your wider role as a PE teacher, in S. Capel (ed.) *Learning to Teach Physical Education in the Secondary School: A Companion to School Experience*, 2nd edn, London: RoutledgeFalmer, pp. 239–58.

USEFUL WEBSITES

BERA (British Educational Research Association) (2000) *Good Practice in Educational Research Writing*, at: http://www.bera.ac.uk/search/archive_view.php?search_term=ethics&url= http://www.bera.ac.uk/beradev2002/root/archive//writing.html (accessed 3 June 2005)

DCMS (Department for Culture, Media and Sport) at: www.culture.gov.uk

DfES (Department for Education and Skills) (2005) at http://www.dfes.gov.uk/keyskills/ what.shtml (accessed 19 April 2005).

DfES (Department for Education and Skills) at http://www.dfes.gov.uk/pess

DfES (Department for Education and Skills) at http://www.standards.dfes.gov.uk/ specialistschools

DfES (Department for Education and Skills) at: http://www.standards.dfes.gov.uk/ schemes2/Secondary_PE

http://www.hants.gov.uk/TC/cg/photoschools.html (accessed 25 May 2005)
http://www.infed.org/biblio/b-reflect.htm
http://www.infed.org/thinkers/et-schon.htm
http://www.nc.uk.net
http://www.rtweb.info
OfSTED (Office for Standards in Education) at http://www.Ofsted.gov.uk
http://www.physical-literacy.org.uk
QCA at http://www.qca.org.uk/ages3-14/afl/295.html
QCA at http://www.qca.org.uk/ages3-14/afl/296.html
QCA at http://www.qca.org.uk/ca/5-14/afl/
Sport England at http://www.sportengland.org/active_schools
Sports Coach UK at http://www.sportscoachuk.org
Youth Sport Trust at http://www.youthsporttrust.org

Subject index

A Level 82
academic learning time – physical education (ALT-PE) 34–5, 92–4
Accelerated Learning 56
accidents 111
achievement of pupils 119–31
action research 28–38; data analysis for 37; data collection for 31–7; ethics of 28–9; how to do 31; identifying focus of 30; plan of action for 32; process of 30; see also data
Acts: Education Reform 73, 121, 131; Education (Schools) 73; Race Relations (Amendment) 131; Revised SEN Code of Practice 131; Sex Discrimination 131
Adults Other Than Teachers (AOTTs) 150, 152
aims of physical education 4–17, 40, 41; extrinsic to physical education; 9–10; intrinsic to physical education 9–10; unique to physical education 9–10; shared with other subjects 9–10
assessment of pupils 12, 133–43; basic strategy 135–7; criteria 139, 141; for learning 133–4; formative 51, 64, 86, 134, 143; of learning 134, 142; planning for 134–38, 142, 143; progress 139; summative 51, 134, 143
athletics; safety and 113; see also physical education curriculum

badminton: see physical education curriculum
basketball: see physical education curriculum
behaviour 90–7; contract 96; inappropriate 97; management of 90, 94, 96; poor 96; of pupils 99
behaviour for learning 90, 94, 96
British Association of Advisers and Lecturers in Physical Education (BAALPE) *Safe Practice in Physical Education and School Sport* 102–3, 110–1, 115–7
British Educational Research Association (BERA) 29

changing room 91
citizenship 12–3; 73
classroom management: see organisation and management
classroom organisation: see organisation and management

confidence as teacher 90, 94–5
connectivity 51
content: of lessons 12, 14, 17; knowledge 22
continuity 46–9, 50
contra-indications 102, 108
Croner *The Head's Legal Guide* 102–3, 116
curriculum 73; broad and balanced 46–8; see also extra-curricular; physical education curriculum

dance animateur 152
dance safety and 113; see also physical education curriculum
data protection 88
data: qualitative 37; quantitative 37; see also action research
debriefing session 23
Department for Education and Employment (DfEE) 42
Department for Education and Skills (DfES) 50, 102
Department of Education and Science and the Welsh Office (DES/WO) 42
Department of National Heritage (DNH) 42
development of teachers 21
differentiation 65–7, 74, 119, 124–30, 134–5, 139
digital cameras 82, 86–7
Director of Sport 152
duty of care 101

Education (Schools) Act 73
Education Reform Act 73, 121, 131
education; relationship of physical education with 4
educational theory 23
effective: learning environment 90–9; practice 28
effectiveness of your teaching 21, 23
equality of opportunity 119, 121–2, 128; access 121, 122; entitlement 121; mixed sex 122, 128; policies 122; principles 121; single sex 122
equipment / resources 91
ethos of physical education 40–1; see also school ethos
evaluation 12, 37; of your teaching 21–3, 28; see also lesson evaluation
experience by teacher 19
experiential learning 56

extra-curricular activities 7–8, 147, 150; safety in 110

feedback 21, 94
football 121, 130; see also physical education curriculum

games safety and 113; see also physical education curriculum
General Certificate of Education (GCE) A Level 82
General Certificate of Secondary Education (GCSE) 82, 87; A Level 82
goals 5, 12, 17; broader educational 9
gymnastics safety and 113; see also physical education curriculum

Health and Safety Executive 110
hockey: see physical education curriculum

improving your teaching 21
in loco parentis 101
inclusion 90, 119, 121, 123, 124; barriers to 121; gifted and talented 130; learning challenges 121; needs 119, 121, 124, 131; segregation 121; Statutory Inclusion Statement 121; teaching styles 124
information and communication technology (ICT) 80–8
intentions of teacher 4, 17
interactions: teacher with pupils 94–5; between pupils 94
interviews (for research) 32–3, 37
invasion games 83

jewellery of pupils 91, 111
justification for physical education in the curriculum 4–12, 41

key skills 12–3, 53, 80–5; application of number 81–4; communication 81–5; improving own learning and performance 81–4; information technology 81–4; problem solving 81–4; working with others 81–4;
Key Stage 3 requirements for physical education 46
Key Stage 4 requirements for physical education 46
Key Stage Strategy 44; Key Stage 3 Strategy 143

language: development through physical education 9; for learning 53
laptop computers 82, 87
learning outcomes 4–17, 19, 21–2, 50–1, 74, 76–7, 83, 85, 124, 128, 133–42; lesson 62–8; unit 54–62
Learning Support Assistant 150
learning: across the curriculum 44; by pupils 21, 30, 73–9, 90, 94; styles 50, 53, 57; see also teaching and learning strategies
legal terms 101
leisure 7–8
lesson: climate 90, 94, 96–9; evaluation 20–1, 134, 139, 142; planning 4, 12, 21, 40, 50, 62–68, 90–1, 94–5, 102; quality 21; see also planning
liability 101
literature review for an action research project 30–3

local education authorities (LEAs) 102

management of pupils 65–6
management: see organisation and management
mobilising activities 107
monitoring of a class 19
motivation of pupils 36–7, 94–5
movement education 7–8
Multiple Intelligences 56

National Curriculum for Physical Education (NCPE) 40, 44, 46, 50, 73, 88, 100, 102, 111, 113, 121, 146–7, 149–50; assessment 73, 133–43; Attainment Target 41; breadth of study 73, 77, 140, 148; general teaching requirements 148; level descriptions 57; levels of attainment 73; NCPE 2000 41; principles 121; Programmes of Study 41, 49, 121; strands of learning 41, 44, 46, 48–9, 50–66, 73, 82, 140; wider demands of 45; see also physical education curriculum
National Key Stage 3 Strategy: see Key Stage Strategy 143
nature of physical education 4–11, 90
negligence 101–2, 111
net and wall games: see physical education curriculum
netball: see physical education curriculum

objectives 4–17, 40
observation: of pupils 19, 32; schedules 32–6; of another teacher 92; of your teaching 21, 92
Office for Standards in Education (OfSTED) 51
Organisation: of equipment 65–7; and management of lessons 12, 90–9
outdoor and adventurous activities (OAA) safety and 113; see also physical education curriculum

PEAUK 115–7
performance targets 21
philosophy of education 17
physical education curriculum 73, 74, 122, 146, 148–53; athletics 127, 129, 139, 140–1; badminton 55, 58, 83; basketball 51; broader dimensions 46–8. 73–9; dance 76, 77, 128, 129, 130, 139, 142, 150; football 121, 130; games 46, 77–8, 82–3, 130; gymnastics 46, 62, 74, 82, 84–5, 104, 128–9, 130, 142; high quality 147; hockey 130; net and wall games 55, 83; netball 121, 134; outdoor and adventurous activity 46, 82, 84, 129; rugby 78, 121, 128–9, 139; school sport 150–1, 153; skills 74–5; striking and fielding games 83; swimming 47, 74, 84, 126–30, 139; techniques 74–5; tennis 73, 75, 83, 130; see also National Curriculum for Physical Education
Physical Education, School Sport and Club Links (PESSCLs) 130, 153
physical education: as an end in itself 9–14; a means to other ends 9–12, 14
planning: 11–2, 16–7, 22; lessons 4, 12, 21, 40, 50, 62–8, 90–1, 94–5, 102; long-term 40–9; medium-term 40, 50–62; short-term 40, 50, 62–8; units of work 40, 50–63, 102
policies: of school 96
powerpoint presentation 87
priorities of teacher 16–7

problem situations 8
progression 46–50
projectors 87
pulse-raising activities 107
punishment 79
pupil learning: see learning by pupils
pupils: ability 119, 121, 128, 134, 139; body shape
    128; clothing 130; culture 119, 128; gender
    119, 121, 128; gifted and talented 119, 130–1;
    groupings 91; needs 119, 121, 124, 131;
    physical maturity 126, 128; race 119, 121, 128;
    religion 119, 121; social skills 77;
    understanding 21; wider 73

Qualification and Curriculum Authority (QCA)
    50–2
qualitative data 37
quantitative data 37
questioning by teacher of pupils 35
questionnaires 32–4, 37

Race Relations (Amendment) Act 131
recreation 6–8
reflection 18–28, 30, 37, 90; in action, on action
    and teaching as a whole 19–23; self-reflection
    16, 18–28; see also teaching: reflective
    approach
reflective practice: see reflection
register 91
relationships: between pupils 95; between
    teacher and pupils 94–5
research: see action research
Revised SEN Code of Practice 131
risk: assessment 115; environmental
    considerations and 114; facilities and 112;
    management 110–115
role, physical education teacher 146–53;
    partnership 148, 150–3
rugby: see physical education curriculum

safe practice 100–17; considerations 109
schemes of work 40, 44, 48–9, 50, 52, 83, 102
school ethos 40–1
school sport 7–8
School Sports Coordinator 152
School Sports Partnerships Programme 150,
    152–3
School Teachers' Pay and Conditions Act 101
self-appraisal 21
self-esteem of pupils 94–5
Sex Discrimination Act 131
skills: of pupils 19; see also key skills, thinking
    skills
social, moral, spiritual, cultural and personal
    development 73–79, 148

society: place of physical education in 4
Specialist Sports College 150, 152, 153
sport 4, 7–8; differences to physical education 4,
    6
Sport England 153
Sports Development Officer 152
SportsCoach UK 153
standards to achieve qualified teacher status
    23
stopwatches 82, 86–7
strategy 22
stretching 107; static 107; dynamic 107; ballistic
    107
striking and fielding games 83; see also physical
    education curriculum
swimming 47, 74, 84, 126–30, 139; safety and 113;
    see also physical education curriculum

targets for pupils 23, 94
teacher: career 23; as a professional 12, 16–7;
    qualities 16–7
teaching 4; approaches 12, 14–5, 17, 30;
    competitive activities 46, 48; facilities 46;
    improving quality of 30; individual activities
    46, 48; integral 76; and learning environment
    28; and learning points 65–7; and learning
    strategies 73, 75, 77–9, 119, 126–8; non-
    competitive activities 46, 48; procedures 104;
    reflective approach to 74–5, 78; routines 104;
    skills 16, 30; strategies 53, 67; style 94–5; team
    activities 46, 48
tennis 73, 75, 83, 130; see also physical education
    curriculum
thinking: reflective by teacher 18–27; skills of
    pupils 12–3
trampolining 111; see also physical education
    curriculum
triangulation (for research) 38

units of work 4, 21, 76, 135, 139; evaluation of 21

validity 32, 34, 38
valuables of pupils 91
value of the subject 16
values 4–5, 11–2, 40, 41
vicarious liability 101
video camera 86
videotape recording 32–4
visual, auditory and kinaesthetic learning (VAC)
    56–7

warm-up 107
working space 94–5

Youth Sport Trust 152

Author index

Abbott, J. with Ryan, T. 80, 81, 88
Arnold, P.J. 10
Ashworth, S. with Mosston, M. 17, 124
Assessment Reform Group 133
Ayres, H. with Gray, F. 99

Baumann, A. with Bloomfield, A. and Roughton, L. 68
Beedy, J.P. 79
Bell, J. 31, 37
Bentley, T. with Gardner, H. 88
Bleach, K. 96
Bloomfield, A. with Baumann, A. 68
Boud, D. with Keogh, R. and Walker, D. 18, 19
British Association of Advisers and Lecturers in Physical Education (BAALPE) 102, 103, 110, 115, 117
British Educational Research Association (BERA) 29
Bryson, J. 99

Capel, S. 11, 49, 88, 139, 143; with Leah, J. 17; with Lawrence, J. 91; with Leask, M. and Turner, T. 99, 124; with Piotrowski, S. 11, 17; with Whitehead, M. and Zwozdiak-Myers, 94; with Zwozdiak-Myers 12, 73, 75, 146
Carr, W. with Kemmis, S. 28
Chandler, T. with Penney, D. 42, 51
Chelsea School 139, 142
Cohen, L. with Manion, L. and Morrison, K. 68
Croner 102, 103, 115, 117

Department for Culture, Media and Sport (DCMS) 130; with DfES 147, 150, 153; with DoH 148
Department for Education (DfE) 96
Department for Education and Employment (DfEE) with QCA 9, 41, 42, 50, 57, 73, 102, 113, 117, 121, 123, 130
Department for Education and Skills (DfES) 68, 80, 130, 131, 132, 133, 134, 143; with DCMS 147, 150, 153; with QCA 50
Department of Education and Science (DES) 9, 46, 73, 121; with the Welsh Office 42, 73
Department of Health (DoH) with DCMS 148
Department of National Heritage (DNH) 42
Dewey, J. 18, 19

Donovan, G. with McNamara, J. and Gianoli, P. 102, 117

Earl, L. with Hargreaves, A. 28
Ebbutt, D. 29, 30
Edmonsdon, G. with Katene, W. 100, 115, 117
Education Reform Act 121, 131
Elbourn, J. with Harris, J. 117
Elliott, J. 30
Erickson, G. with Grimmett, P. 19
Evans, J. 132; with Penney, D. 4Talbot, M. 422

Gardner, H. 56, with Bentley, T. 88
Garner, P. 90, 94, 99
Gianoli, P. with Donovan, G. 102, 117
Gray, F. with Ayres, H. 99
Grey, J. with Hopper, B. 117
Griffey, D.C. with Housner, L.D. 64
Grimmett, P. with Erickson, G. 19

Hargreaves, A. with Earl, L., Moore, S. and Manning, S. 28
Harris, J. with Elbourn, J. 117
Hayes, S. with Stidder, G. 132
Health and Safety Executive (HSE) 110, 117
Hepworth, N. with Shenton, P. 150
Hopkins, D. 28, 29, 33
Hopper, B. with Grey, J. and Maude, P. 117
Housner, L.D. with Griffey, D.D. 64

Katene, W. with Edmondson, G. 100, 115, 117
Kemmis, S. 29, 30; with Carr, W. 28
Keogh, R. with Boud, D. 18, 19
Kolb, D. 56
Kyriacou, C. 23, 27

Laker, A. 79
Lawrence, J. with Taylor, A. and Capel, S. ; with Whitehead, M. and Capel, S. 91
Leah, J. with Capel, S. 17
Leask, M. 17; with Capel, S. 17, 99, 124
Lockwood, A. with Newton, A. 143
Loughran, J. 18

Macintyre, C. 31
Manion, L. with Cohen, L. 68
Manning, S. with Hargreaves, A. 28

Maude, P. with Hopper, B. 117
McKernan, J. 28, 29, 30
McNamara, J. with Donovan, G. 102, 117
Moore, A. 23, 27, 28
Moore, S. with Hargreaves, A. 28
Morrison, K. with Cohen, L. 68
Mosston, M. with Ashworth, S. 17, 124
Munby, H. with Russell, T. 19
Murdoch, E. 42, 46, 49, 148

Newton, A. with Lockwood, A. 143
Norris, C.M. 102, 117

Office for Standards in Education (OfSTED) 46, 51

Parker, M. with Siedentop, D. 34, 35, 93
PEAUK 115, 117
Penney, D. 42; with Chandler, T. 42, 51; with Evans, J. 42
Piotrowski, S. with Capel, S. 11, 17
Pollard, A. with Triggs, P. 68

Qualifications and Curriculum Authority (QCA) 52, 134; with DfEE 9, 41, 42, 50, 57, 73, 102, 113, 117, 121, 123, 130; with DfES 50

Race Relations (Amendment) Act 131
Raymond, C. 100, 115, 117, 118
Rink, J.E. 124
Robson, C. 37
Rose, C. 56
Roughton, L. with Baumann, A. 68
Runneymede Trust 132
Russell, T. with Munby, H. 19
Ryan, T. with Abbott, J. 80, 81, 88

Schon, D. 18, 19
Severs, J. with Whitlam, P. and Woodhouse, J. 100, 115, 118
Sex Discrimination Act 131
Shenton, P. with Hepworth, N. 150
Siedentop, D. with Toussignant, M. and Parker, M. 34, 35, 93
Special Needs and Disability Act 131
Stidder, G. 88, 139; with Hayes, S. 132

Talbot, M. 42
The Office for Standards in Education (OfSTED) 46, 51
The School Teachers' Pay and Conditions Act 101
Theodoulides, A. 73
Toussignant, M. with Siedentop, D. 34, 35, 93
Triggs, P. with Pollard, A. 68
Turner, T. with Capel, S. 17, 99, 124

Vickerman, P. 121, 124

Walker, D. with Boud, D. 18, 19
Weare, K. 94
Welsh Office with DES 42
Whitehead, M. 4, 5, 11; with Capel, S. 94; with Lawrence, J. 91; with Zwozdiak-Myers, P. 12, 73, 75, 77, 146
Whitlam, P. 100, 115, 118; with Severs, J. 100, 115, 118
Woodhouse, J. with Severs, P. 100, 115, 118

Zwozdiak-Myers, P. with Capel, S. 94; with Whitehead, M. 12, 77; with Whitehead, M. and Capel, S. 12, 73, 75, 146